The Egg

Name _____

Cut out the butterfly.
Cut out the egg.
Paste them on the milkweed leaf.

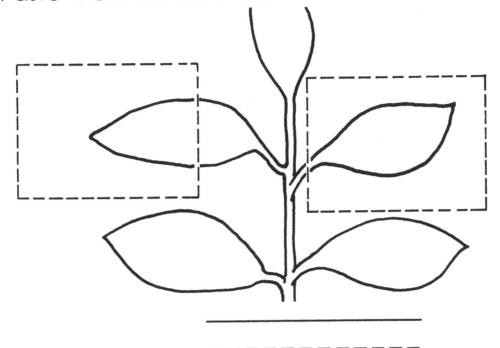

_____
- - - - - - - - - - - - - - -

The butterfly lays one _____ on a milkweed

_____
- - - - - - - - - - - - -
_____ .

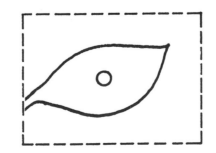

Word Bank

leaf

egg

The Caterpillar

Name _____

Cut out the caterpillar.
Paste it on the milkweed leaf.
Color the caterpillar black, white, and yellow.

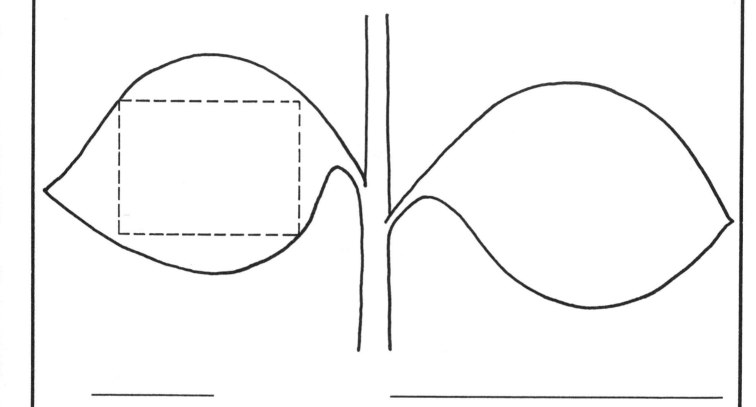

_____   _____

- - - - - - -   - - - - - - - - - - - - - -

The _____ hatches into a _____.

Word Bank

egg
caterpillar

Growing

Cut out the caterpillar and its food.
Paste them on the milkweed plant.

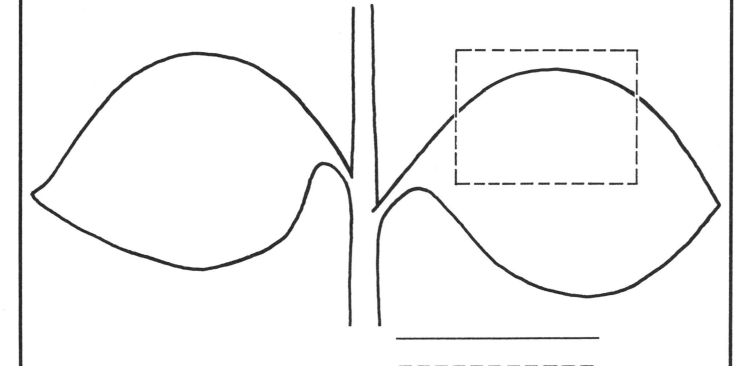

The hungry caterpillar eats the _____ .

The caterpillar is _____ .

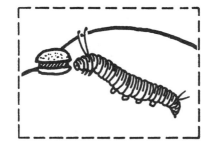 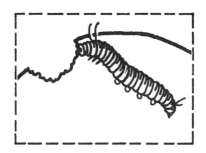

Word Bank

leaf

growing

The Chrysalis

Name _____

Cut out the chrysalis.
Paste it in place.

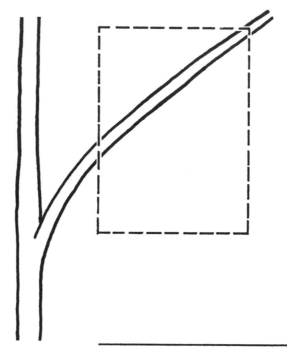

_____

- - - - - - - - - - - - - - - - - - -

The caterpillar is ready to _____.

_____

- - - - - - - - - - - - - - - - -

It forms a pale _____ chrysalis.

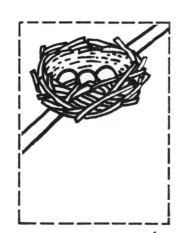

Word Bank

green
change

IF8757 Science Enrichment

The Butterfly

Name _____

Cut out the butterfly.
Paste it in place.

The _____ is now a butterfly.

The _____ flies away.

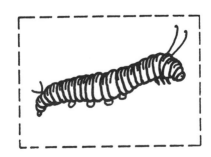

Word Bank

butterfly
caterpillar

IF8757 Science Enrichment

Metamorphosis

Name _____

Show how the monarch changes.
Cut out the pictures.
Paste them in order.

Word Bank
butterfly

_____

The life cycle of a _____
is called metamorphosis.

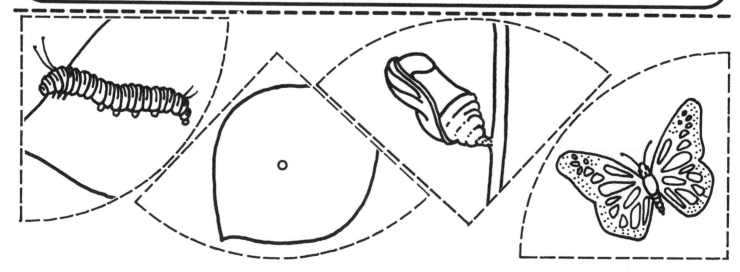

Insects

Cut out the monarch butterfly.
Paste it in place.
Color just the insects.

The monarch butterfly is an _____ .

_____
- - - - - - - - - - - - - - - - - -
It has six _____ .

_____
- - - - - - - - - - - - - - - - - - - -
It has _____ body parts.

Word Bank

insect
three
legs

the Butterfly

by _____

IF8757 Science Enrichment

Migration

Name _____

Cut out the animals.
Paste them in place.

_____
It is hard to find _____ in the winter.

_____
It is hard to stay _____ in the winter.

Some animals move to warmer places then.
This is called migration.

Word Bank
warm
food

IF8757 Science Enrichment

Active Animals

Name _____

Cut out the animals.
Paste them in place.

It is winter.
Deep snow covers the ground.

Some animals can find _____.

Some animals can stay _____.

These animals stay active in winter.

Word Bank

food

warm

Storing Food

Name _____

Cut out the beaver.
Paste him by the hole in the ice.
Trace the path to the beaver's lodge.

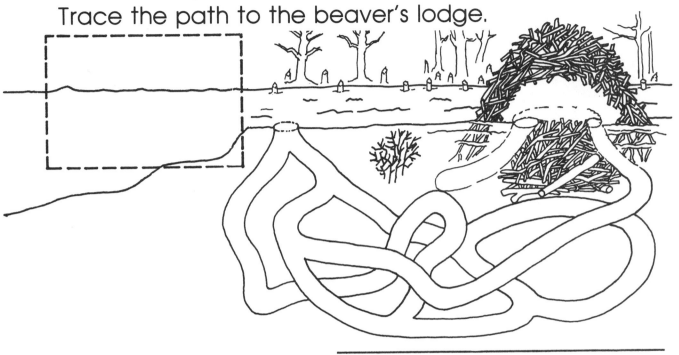

_____
- -

Some animals store food for _____ .

_____
- -

The beaver stores food in his _____ .

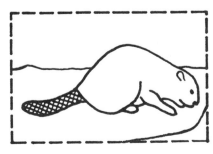   

Word Bank
lodge
winter

IF8757 Science Enrichment

Hibernation

Name _____

Cut out the fat woodchuck.
Paste him by his hole.
Trace the path to the
woodchuck's home.

Some animals hibernate in the winter.

_____

The woodchuck grows a layer of _____ in the fall.

_____

His heartbeat goes_____. His temperature goes

_____   _____

_____. He stays in his home while it is _____.

Word Bank
cold
fat
down
down

Animals in Winter

Name _____

Cut out the animal.
Paste it in its place.
Write the animal's name.

This animal hibernates in the winter.
_____
- - - - - - - - - - - - - - - - - - - -
_____

This animal migrates in the winter.
_____
- - - - - - - - - - - - - - - - - - - -
_____

This animal stays active in the winter.
_____
- - - - - - - - - - - - - - - - - - - -
_____

This animal stores food for the winter.
_____
- - - - - - - - - - - - - - - - - - - -
_____

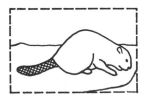   

Word Bank

rabbit
bird
beaver
woodchuck

Animals in Winter

by _____

Frogs

Name _____

Cut out the frogs.
Paste the big frog on the lily pad.
Paste the little frog on the log.
Trace the path from the log to the lily pad.

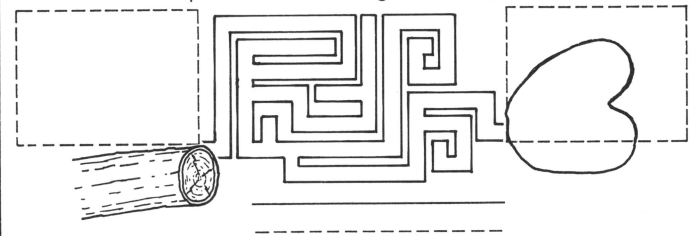

Frogs can live in the _____ .

Frogs can live on _____ .

_____ are amphibians.

Word Bank
land
water
frogs

IF8757 Science Enrichment

Laying Eggs

Name _____

Cut out the frog's eggs.
Paste them in the water.

The frog lays her _____ in the spring.

She lays the eggs in the _____ .

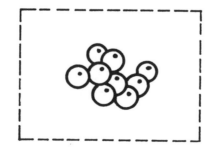

Word Bank
water
eggs

Tadpoles

Name _____

Cut out the tadpole.
Paste it in the water.

The eggs hatch into _____ .

They breathe with _____ like fish.

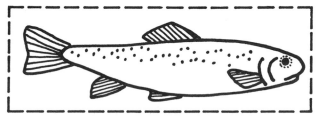

Word Bank
gills
tadpoles

Growing

Name _____

Cut out the changing tadpole.
Paste it in the water.

_____
- - - - - - - - - - - - -

The tadpole grows _____ .

_____
- - - - - - - - - - - - -

Its _____ becomes smaller.

_____
- - - - - - - - - - - - - - - -

The tadpole still lives in the _____ .

_____
- - - - - - - - - - - -

It can live on land when it becomes a _____ .

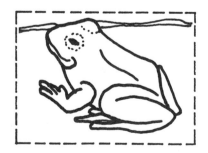 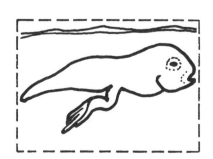

Word Bank

tail
water
legs
frog

IF8757 Science Enrichment

The Life Cycle of a Frog

Name _____

Cut out the pictures.
Paste them in order.
Write the name of each picture.

Word Bank
egg
adult
tadpole

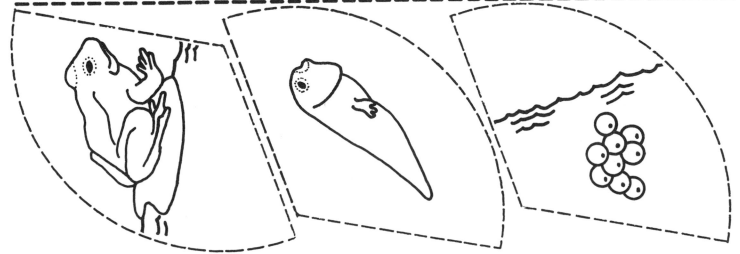

The Frog

by _____

IF8757 Science Enrichment

Tree Parts

Name _____

Trees have three main parts. They are the trunk, the roots, and the leaves. Each part has a special job. Each part helps the tree.

Cut out the name of each part.
Cut out the job of each part.
Paste them on the picture.
Color the tree.

Name

Job

trunk	leaves	roots

I hold the tree in the ground.	I make food for the tree.	I hold most of the tree above the ground.

Leaf Shapes

All leaves are not the same. They have different shapes. There are four common shapes.

Draw a line to match the leaf with its shape.

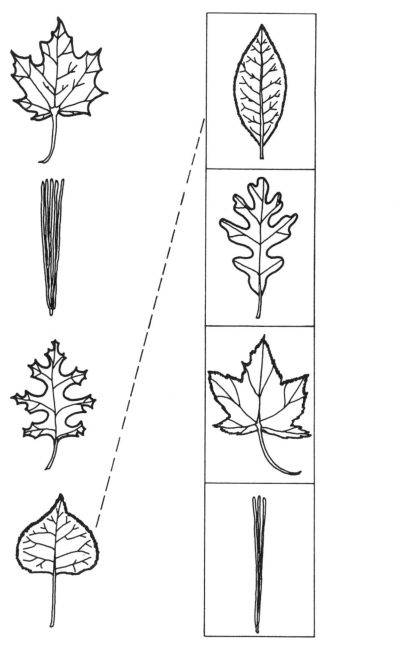

Find some leaves outside.
Try to match them to the shapes.

Leaf Study

Name _____

Put a leaf under the box on this paper. Rub the paper with the side of your crayon. Use the ruler at the bottom to measure your leaf.

This is a rubbing of my leaf.

1. The color of my leaf is _____ .

2. My leaf is _____ cm wide and _____ cm long.

3. My leaf feels like _____ .

4. I found my leaf _____ .

 IF8757 Science Enrichment

Food Factories

Name _____

Green leaves are like little factories. They make food for the tree. Leaves need sunshine, air, and water to make food.

Leaves change in the fall. They lose their green color. Then they cannot make food for the tree.

Draw a leaf.
This leaf can make food.
Color it green.

Draw another leaf.
This leaf cannot make food.
Color it with pretty fall colors.

Write the correct word.

green yellow
_____

Food is made by _____ leaves.

shade sunshine
_____

Leaves need _____ to make food.

can cannot
_____

Leaves _____ make food in the fall.

My Leaf Collection

Attach a leaf and fill in the blanks.

Teacher: Provide each student with three or more copies of this page so booklets can be made.

Tree _____

Location _____

Date _____

Tree Seeds

Name _____

Some trees drop their seeds in the spring. Other trees drop their seeds in the fall. The seeds grow up. Do you know what they grow up to be?

Show how the acorn grows into a mighty oak tree. Write first, second, or third under the pictures to put them in order. Color the pictures.

Finish the story.
I am a little acorn. One day

Trees Change

Some trees do not look the same all year long. Their leaves are not always the same. These trees change with each season.

Color the tree to show how it will look each season.

Spring

Summer

Fall

Winter

Trees Are Different

Name _____

    Some trees change with the seasons. Other trees do not change with the seasons. They stay green all year long. These trees are called evergreens.

    Color the trees to show how they are different each season.

 Spring

 Summer

 Fall

 Winter

 IF8757 Science Enrichment

Trees Give Us Food

Name _____

People can eat the food from trees. Animals can also eat the food from trees. The food comes from different parts of the tree.

Label the foods that people get from trees.

![apple]	![corn]	![cherries]
_____	_____	_____
![cabbage]	![nut]	![pear]
_____	_____	_____

Label the foods that animals get from trees.

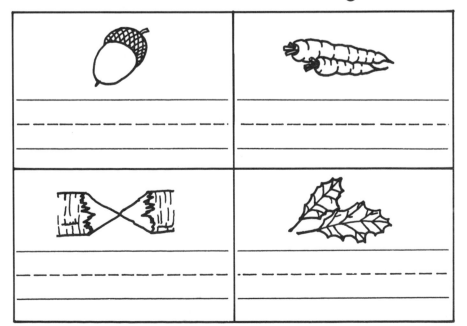

Word Bank

apple
corn
cherries
cabbage
nut
pear
acorn
carrot
bark
leaves

I'm a Tree

Name _____

Write the answer to each riddle in the puzzle.

Across

4. I'm left over after a fire.
5. Part of me can be used to make bouncing balls.
6. My fruit is very sour.
7. I am either green or black.
8. George Washington chopped me down.

Down

1. I make great syrup.
2. Many drink my fruit's juice for breakfast.
3. Some say I keep the doctor away.

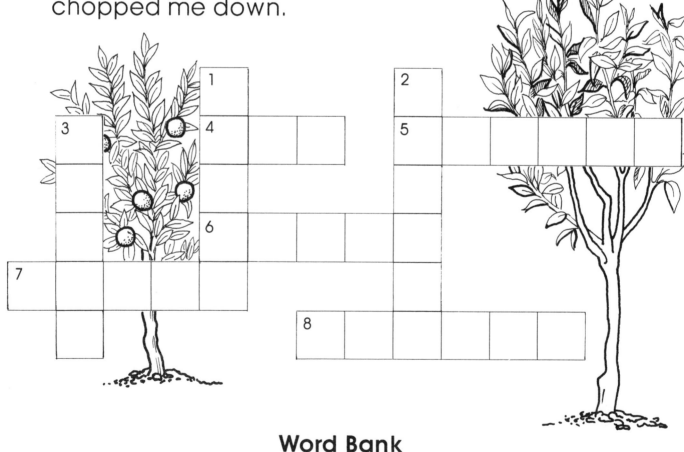

Word Bank

cherry   olive   lemon   rubber
ash   apple   maple   orange

Trees Help Us

Name _____

Trees are used in many ways. Sometimes we eat the food from trees. Sometimes we build things with the wood from trees. Can you name some tree products?

Draw a line from the tree products to the tree. Circle the tree products.

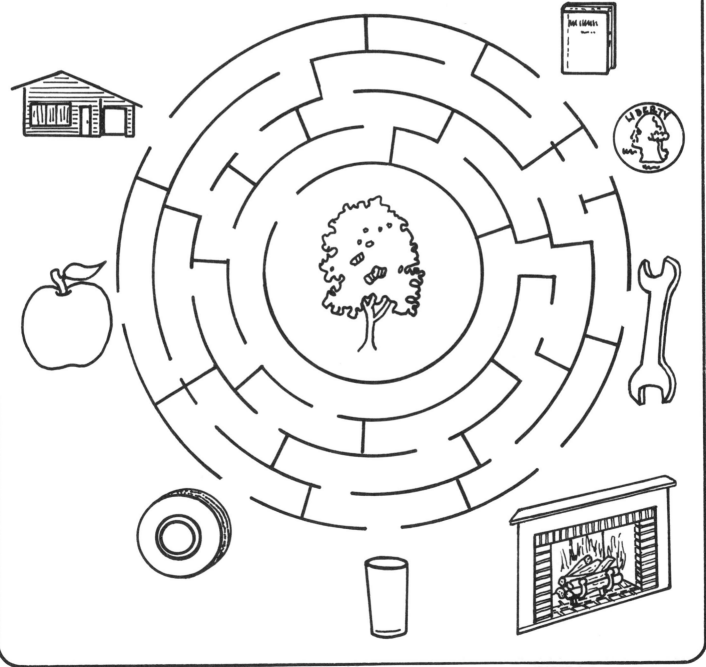

 IF8757 Science Enrichment

Sugar Bush

Name _____

Spring is maple syrup time. People collect the sap from maple trees. They boil the sap until it becomes maple syrup. It takes thirty gallons of sap to make one gallon of syrup.

Color the pictures.
Write numbers next to the pictures in the order that maple syrup is made.

Many Kinds of Trees

Name _____

There are many kinds of trees. Each kind has a different name. Can you name some trees?

Circle the hidden trees.

```
O A K
A P P L E
P E C A N U L G H T
X Y O X S P R U C E
W A L N U T Z O M T
H B R W O R A N G E
C H E R R Y L E R X
B T R O L X P I N E
C E D A R H M T E R
```

Word Bank
oak
apple
cherry
pine
walnut
cedar
spruce
orange
pecan

Some of the trees above are fruit trees. Some are nut trees. Some are evergreen trees.

Write the tree names that belong in each list.

Fruit	Nut	Evergreen
_____	_____	_____
_____	_____	_____
_____	_____	_____

Plant Parts

Name _____

A plant has many parts. Each part has a special job.

Word Bank   roots   stem
                flower   leaf

Label the parts of the plant.

_____

– – – – – – – – – – – – –

_____

_____

– – – – – – – – – – – – –

_____

_____

– – – – – – – – – – – – –

_____

_____

– – – – – – – – – – – – –

_____

Draw a line from the plant part to its job.

I make the seeds. ●

I make food for the plant. ●

I take water from the roots to the leaves. ●

I hold the plant in the ground. ●

Color the roots red.
Color the stem yellow.
Color the leaves green.
Color the flower your favorite color.

We Eat Plants

Name _____

We eat many foods. Some foods come from animals. Some foods come from plants.

Label the foods we get from plants. Color the foods we get from plants.

Word Bank

banana   carrot
bread   cabbage
apple   corn

We Eat
Plant Parts

Name _____

We eat many plant parts. Sometimes we eat just the fruit. Sometimes we eat just the leaves. We also might eat the stem, the root, or the seed.

Draw a line from the picture to the name of the plant part.

Color the plant part.

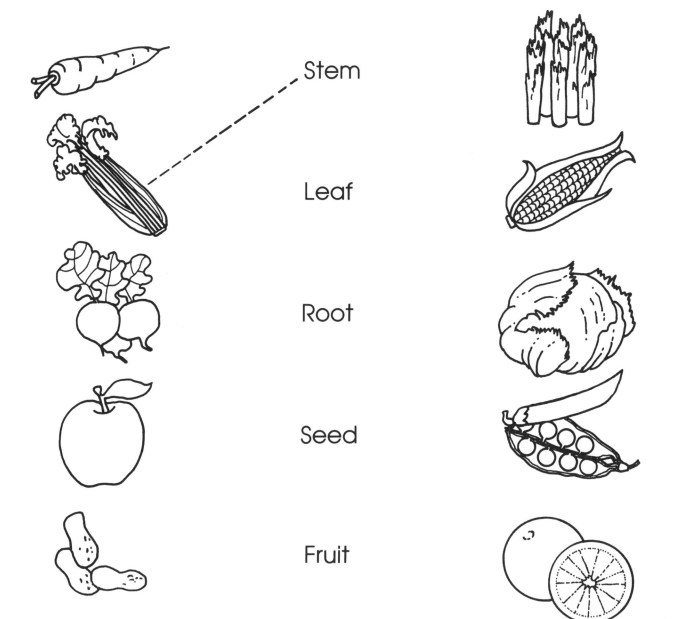

Stem

Leaf

Root

Seed

Fruit

Growing Plants

Name _____

Color the pictures.

Cut them out.

Staple the pictures together.

Put the pictures in order on top of each other.

The youngest plant should be on the top.

Flip the pages and watch the plant grow.

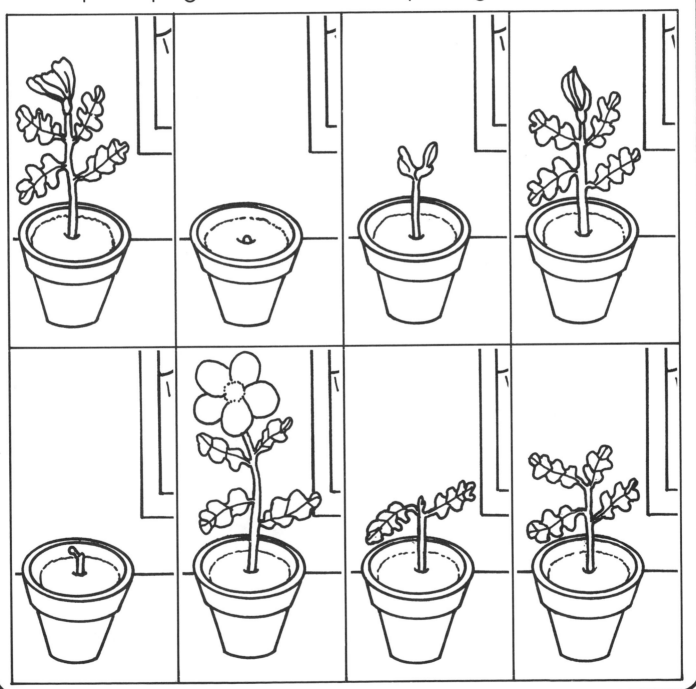

Plants Need Sunshine

Name _____

Mr. Right and Mr. Wrong planted gardens. Mr. Right planted his garden in the sun. Mr. Wrong planted his garden in the shade. Both of them gave their gardens love and care.

Draw what Mr. Right's garden will look like.

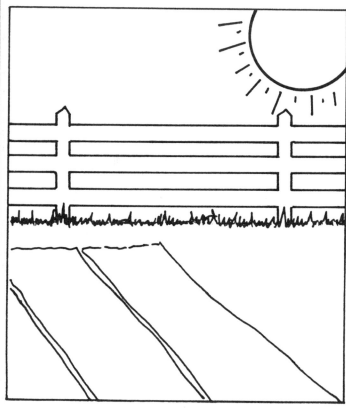

Draw what Mr. Wrong's garden will look like.

Plants Need Water

Name _____

Mrs. Right planted her flower seeds last week. She planted them in the sun. She gave her flowers water.

Draw what Mrs. Right's flowers will look like.

Mrs. Wrong planted her flower seeds last week. She planted them in the sun. But she forgot to give them water.

Draw what Mrs. Wrong's flowers will look like.

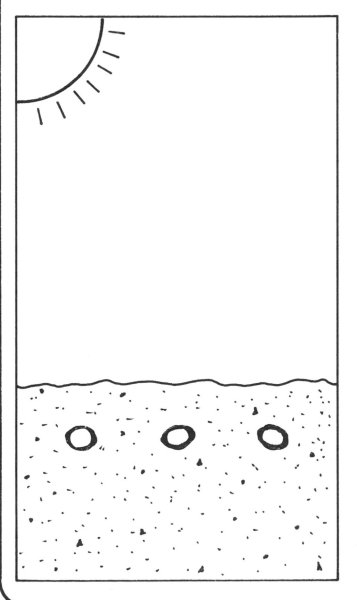

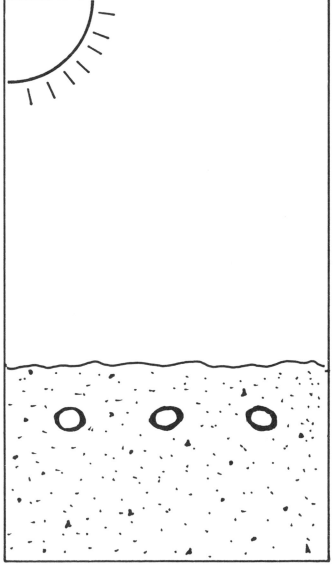

Plants Have Seeds

Name _____

Seeds are found in different parts of the plant. Some seeds are found in the flower. Some seeds are found in the fruit or the nut.

Circle the part of the plant that has the seed. Write the name of the seed.

Word Bank
pine
apple
corn
maple
acorn
dandelion

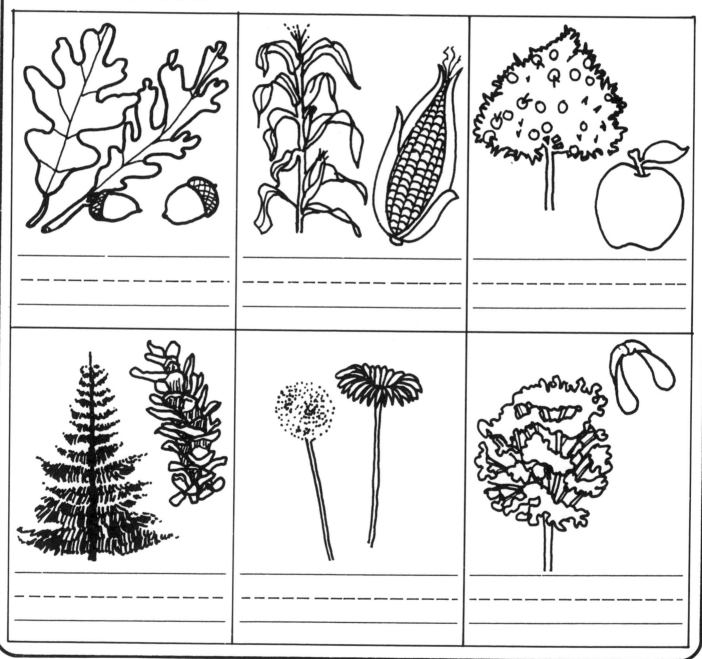

Seeds Travel

Name _____

Seeds travel from one place to another. Sometimes people move the seeds. Sometimes they are moved in other ways.

Finish the sentences to tell how seeds travel.

Word Bank

people
animals
animals
wind
water

Seeds travel with _____.

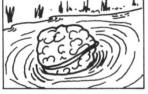

Seeds travel in _____.

Seeds travel on _____.

Seeds travel in _____.

Seeds travel in the _____.

How Many Seeds?

Name _____

Plants have seeds. Some plants have one seed. Other plants have many seeds. When the seeds are planted, they grow into new plants.

Write the name of the plant.
Count the seeds.
Draw a line from the seed to its plant.

_____

_____ seeds

_____

_____ seeds

_____

_____ seed

_____

_____ seeds

Plant Puzzle

Name _____

Use what you have learned about plants and trees to do this puzzle.

Word Bank
roots
seeds
trunk
sun
green

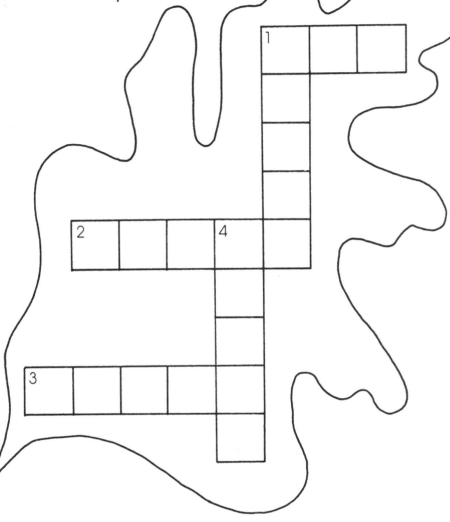

Across
1. Plants and trees need light from the _____ to grow.
2. The _____ hold plants and trees in the ground.
3. Leaves must be _____ to make food for plants and trees.

Down
1. Little _____ grow up to be plants and trees.
4. Most of the tree is held above the ground by the _____.

Animal or Plant

Name _____

All of the foods that we eat come from animals and plants.

Color all of the foods that come from plants.

carrot

egg

grapes

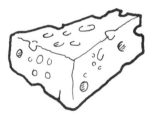

cheese

lettuce

chicken

banana

apple

fish

corn

ice cream

steak

All in the Family

Put an **X** on the animal that does not belong.

1.
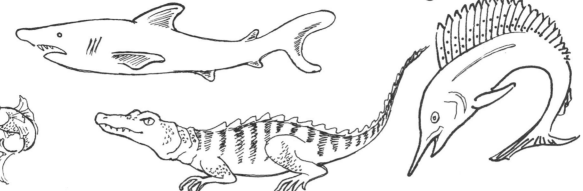

2.

3.

4.

5.

I'm Bigger than You

Name _____

Color the pictures and cut them out.

Glue them in order on a sheet of paper from smallest to largest.

Animals on the Go!

Name _____

How do these animals move?

Write **walk**, **fly** or **swim**.

_____

_____

_____

_____

_____

_____

_____

_____

_____

IF8757 Science Enrichment

At Home in the Pond Community

Name _____

Many animals make their homes in a pond community, but some of the animals in this picture do not belong.

Draw an **X** on the animals that do **not** belong.

At Home in the Grassland Community

Name _____

Many animals make their homes in a grassland community, but some of the animals in this picture do not belong.

Draw an **X** on the animals that do **not** belong.

At Home in the Ocean Community

Name _____

Many animals make their homes in an ocean community, but some of the animals in this picture do not belong.

Draw an **X** on the animals that do **not** belong.

At Home in the Forest Community

Name _____

Many animals make their homes in a forest community, but some of the animals in this picture do not belong.

Draw an **X** on the animals that do **not** belong.

Animals at Home

Name _____

Did you ever see a fish living in a tree? Of course you didn't! Fish live in the water. Help the animals find their homes.

Cut out each animal.
Paste it on its home.
Color the picture.

squirrel   robin   fish   bee

52

Young Animals

Name _____

Many young animals look like their parents. But some do not look like their parents.

Draw a line from the parent to its young.

Write the name of the young.

_____
- - - - - - - - - - - - - - -
_____

_____
- - - - - - - - - - - - - - -
_____

_____
- - - - - - - - - - - - - - -
_____

_____
- - - - - - - - - - - - - - -
_____

Word Bank

kitten   lamb   calf   puppy

Food Chain

Name _____

   The living things on this page are all part of a food chain. A food chain is the order in which living things get their energy. This food chain begins with energy from the sun.

   Cut out the living things.

   Paste them in order on the food chain.

Links in a Chain

Name _____

There are many kinds of living things on this page. You can make a model food chain using the pictures.

1. Color the pictures below and cut them out.
2. Glue each picture to a 2-x-10-inch strip of paper.
3. Make a chain with the strips of paper in the order of a food chain.

Animal Boxes

Name _____

In each box, write the name of two animals that fit the description.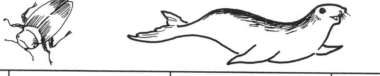

insect	lays eggs	has no legs	has feathers
lives in water	farm animal	has a hard shell	has wings
runs fast	has horns or antlers	has scales	very slow
very strong	has hair	has long legs	is a good pet

	butterfly	cow	horse	clam	
giraffe	elephant	robin	beetle	cat	
snail	turkey	deer	seal	bat	
fish	bee	goat	moose	lion	
turtle	pig	lizard	whale	hawk	

My Bird List

Name _____

Bird watchers keep a list of all the different kinds of birds they have seen. They also keep track of the date and location. Begin a list of your own using the chart below.

Bird	Date	Location

Feathered Friends

Name _____

Name the parts of the bird.

_____

_____

_____

Read the riddle. Name each bird part.

I keep a bird warm and dry. What am I? _____

I help a bird stand or swim. What am I? _____

I help a bird eat. What am I? _____

I make a bird fly high in the sky. What am I? _____

Word Bank			
feathers	feet	bill	wings

Birds

Name _____

Do the puzzle about birds.
Color only the birds.

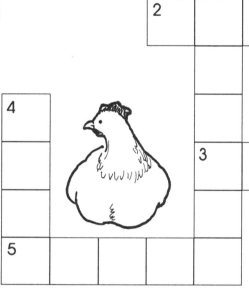

Down

1. _____ keep a bird's body warm and dry.
4. A bird uses its _____ to pick up food.

Across

2. A bird is a _____ -blooded animal.
3. Baby birds are hatched from _____ .
5. Birds breathe with their _____ .

Word Bank				
feathers	bill	lungs	eggs	warm

Reptiles

Name _____

Do the puzzle about reptiles.
Color only the reptiles.

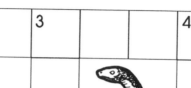

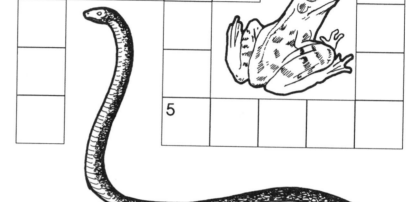

Across

2. A reptile's skin has _____ .

5. A _____ is a reptile with no legs.

Down

1. A _____ is a reptile with a hard shell on its back.

3. Reptiles are _____ -blooded animals.

4. Baby reptiles hatch from _____ .

Word Bank				
eggs	cold	scales	snake	turtle

Amphibians

Name _____

Do the puzzle about amphibians.
Color only the amphibians.

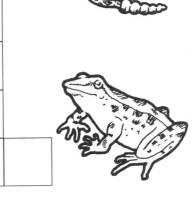
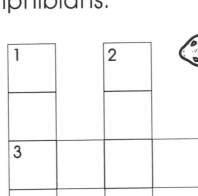

Down

1. Amphibian babies usually hatch from _____.

2. Amphibians are _____ -blooded animals.

4. Amphibians often have smooth, moist _____.

Across

3. Amphibian babies breathe with either lungs or

_____.

5. Amphibians live in the water and on _____.

Word Bank				
land	gills	skin	eggs	cold

Mammals

Name _____

Do the puzzle about mammals.
Color only the mammals.

Down

1. Mammals are _____ -blooded.
4. Mammals breathe with _____ .

Across

2. A mammal's body is usually covered with _____ .
3. Mother mammals feed _____ to their babies.
5. Mammal's _____ are born alive.

Word Bank				
hair	babies	lungs	milk	warm

Fish

Name _____

Do the puzzle about fish.
Color only the fish.

Down

1. Fish have _____ , not legs.
3. A fish's body is often covered with _____ .

Across

2. Fish breathe through _____ .
4. A fish is a _____ -blooded animal.
5. Fish live in the sea and fresh _____ .

Word Bank				
water	scales	cold	fins	gills

Insects

Name _____

Do the puzzle about insects.
Color only the insects.

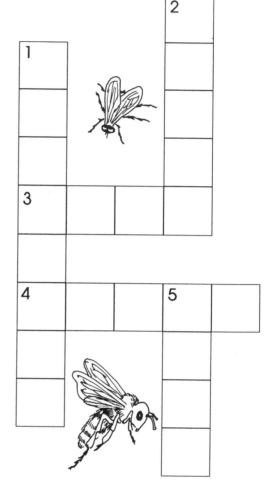

Down
1. Insects have a hard outer _____ .
2. Many insects have two pairs of _____ .
5. Insects have simple and compound _____ .

Across
3. Insects have three pairs of _____ .
4. Insects have _____ main body sections.

Word Bank				
skeleton	legs	wings	three	eyes

IF8757 Science Enrichment

Bones Give You Shape

Name _____

Bones give your body shape. They let you stand up tall. You cannot see your bones. But you can feel many of your bones under your skin

Draw a line from each bone to the part of the body where it is found. Write the name of the bone(s).

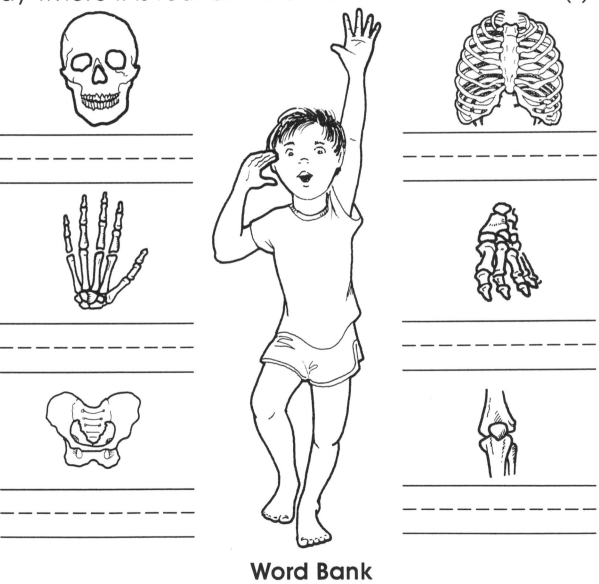

Word Bank

skull	ribs	foot
hand	knee	hips

Name That Bone

Name _____

Name these bones of your skeleton.

_____

_____

_____

_____

_____

_____

_____

_____

_____

Bone Bank

hipbone	arm bone	backbone	rib
collarbone	breastbone	leg bone	skull
knee bone	shoulder blade		

Mr. Bones

(Use with page 68.)

Name _____

Hi, my name is Mr. Bones. This is my skeleton. It gives me my shape. It helps my body move. It also protects my heart, lungs and brain from injury.

1. Cut out my bones.
2. Put them together with brads, matching the letters, A to A, etc.

Bone Bank

ribs	skull	backbone	hipbone
ankle	leg bone	knee bone	collarbone

Mr. Bones
(Continued)

Name _____

Use with page 67.

A

B

C

D

E

D E

D E

Crossbones

Name _____

Across

3. protects your heart and lungs
6. all of your bones
7. connects your leg and foot

Down

1. on the end of your hands
2. on the end of your feet
4. spine
5. makes your leg bend
6. protects your brain

Bone Chest

ribs   toes   fingers

knee   skull   backbone

ankle   skeleton

Eating Good Food

Name _____

The food you eat takes a long trip through your body through your digestive system. Foods are broken down during the journey. The nutrients from the food give your body energy to work and grow.

Color the parts of your digestive system.

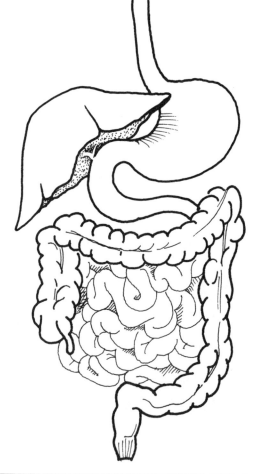

esophagus — yellow

stomach — red

small intestine — blue

large intestine — green

liver — brown

Inside Me
(Part 1)

Name _____

If you could look under your skin, what would you find? You would find muscles, bones, a heart, a brain and many other body parts. Make a model of your insides to show where many of these parts are found.

You will need a friend to help you with the first step of your project.

1. Lay on your back on a large sheet of butcher paper. Turn your head so you are looking over your left shoulder.

2. Have your friend trace your outline with a pencil.

3. Use a dark crayon or marker and trace boldly over the penciled outline.

4. Follow the directions on the following pages.

Optional: You may cut out two body shapes. Glue the body parts on one shape. Staple the other shape underneath it, leaving an opening. Stuff the body with crumpled newspaper to make a 3-D model of you. Finish stapling.

Inside Me—My Brain
(Part 2)

Name _____

My brain has a very important job. It must keep my body working day and night. My brain has three parts.

The **cerebrum** is the largest part of my brain. It does my thinking.

The **cerebellum** makes my muscles move smoothly.

The **brain stem** controls my breathing and the beating of my heart.

1. Color the brain gray.
2. Cut out the brain
3. Glue the brain to your paper body.

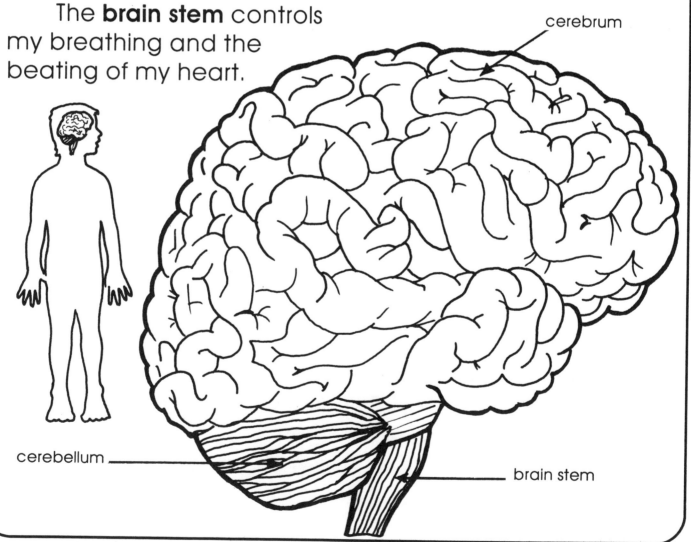

cerebrum

cerebellum

brain stem

Inside Me—Stomach

(Part 3)

Name _____

My stomach is a kind of bag. It can hold about two pints of food. Food travels from my mouth to my stomach through a long tube, called the esophagus. Stomach juices mix with food to help digestion.

My stomach is found on the left side of my body. It is protected by my five lower ribs.

1. Color your stomach blue.

2. Cut out your stomach and glue it to your paper body.

3. Draw a food tube (esophagus) from your stomach to your mouth. Color the food tube brown.

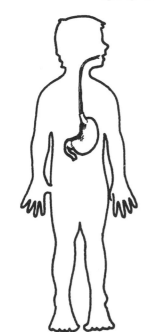

Inside Me—Intestines

(Part 4)

Name _____

Food is broken down in my small intestine. The nutrients are carried away by the blood in millions of small tubes. The leftover waste goes through my large intestine and out my body.

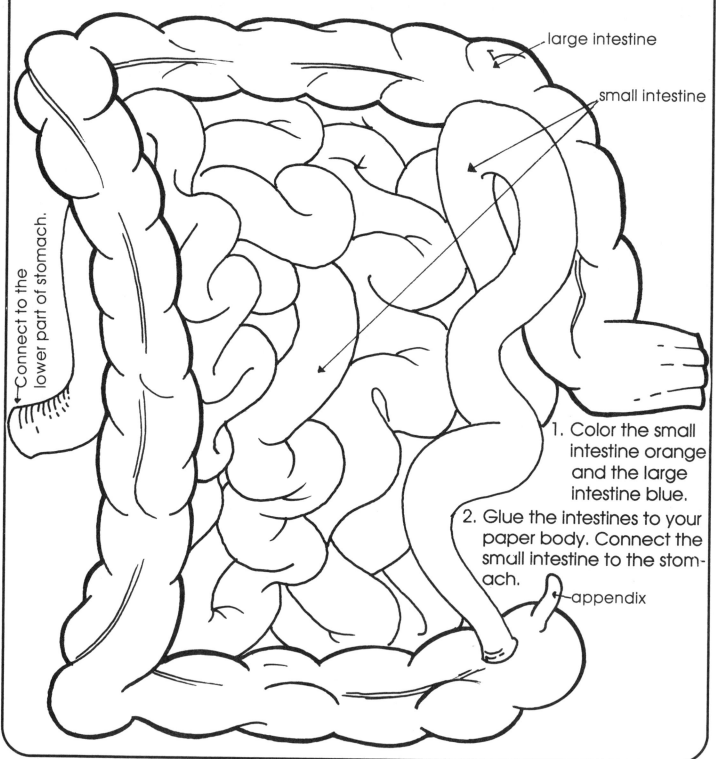

large intestine

small intestine

Connect to the lower part of stomach.

1. Color the small intestine orange and the large intestine blue.

2. Glue the intestines to your paper body. Connect the small intestine to the stomach.

appendix

IF8757 Science Enrichment

Inside Me—Heart
(Part 5)

My heart is a very strong pump. It pumps blood through more than 80,000 miles of tubes (arteries and veins) in my body. My heart is not very big. It is about the size of my fist and weighs less than one pound.

1. Color the heart red.

2. Cut out the heart. Fold and glue the tabs to your paper body.

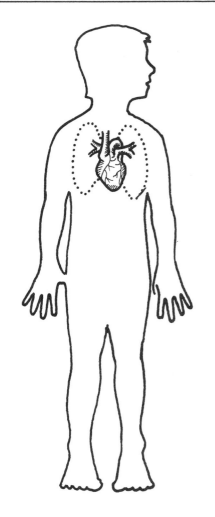

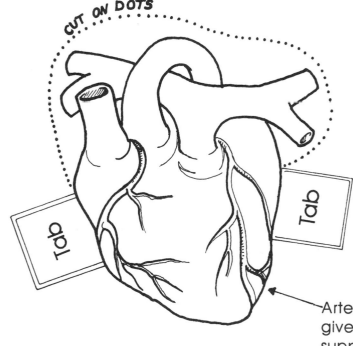

CUT ON DOTS

Tab

Tab

Arteries and veins give the heart its own supply of blood.

Inside Me—Lungs
(Part 6)

Name _____

My lungs take in the air that I breathe and give it to my blood. My blood takes it to all the cells in my body.

1. Color the windpipe and bronchus blue and the lungs red on pages 76 and 77.

2. Cut out the lungs on both pages.

3. Glue the left lung to the right lung on Tab A.

4. Bend and glue both Tabs B to the paper body. (Glue only the tabs.)

5. Draw a windpipe from the lungs to the mouth.

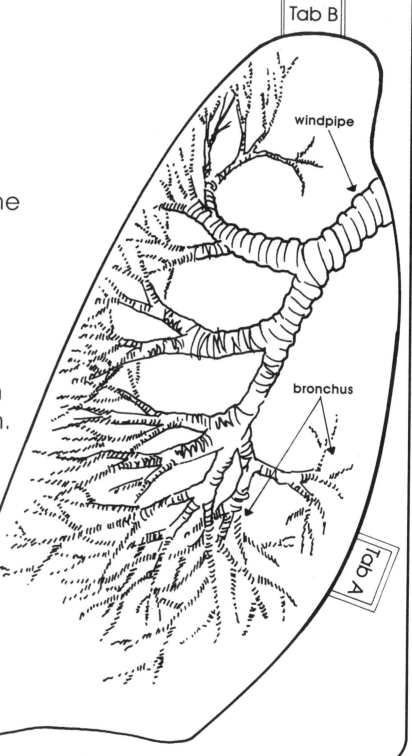

Tab B

windpipe

bronchus

Tab A

Inside Me—Lungs
(Part 6 - continued)

Name _____

Tab B

windpipe→

bronchus

Tab A

Inside Me—Bones
(Part 7)

My bones are very important. My leg bones and arm bones help me move. My skull and ribs protect the soft organs inside my body. Some of my bones make new blood cells for my body.

1. Color the bones yellow.

2. Glue them to your right arm.

Inside Me—Muscles
(Part 8)

Name _____

My muscles make my body move. They are connected to my bones with tendons. One muscle helps my arm bend and the other one helps to straighten it out.

1. Color the muscles red.

2. Cut out and glue the muscles to the bones on the right arm.

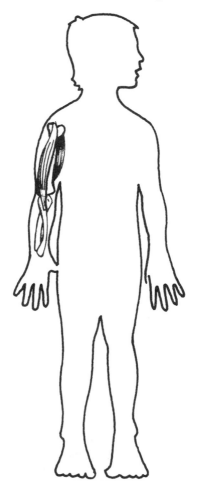

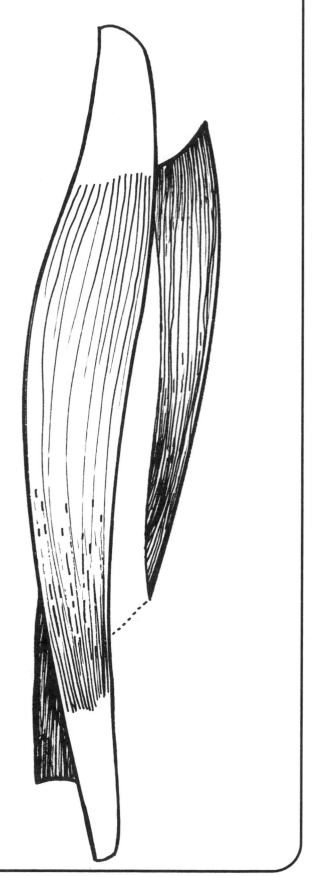

Body Language

Name _____

Circle the words that are part of your body.

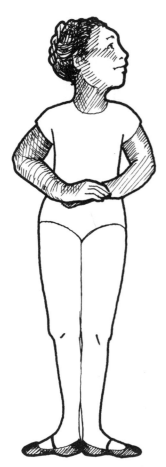

a	t	e	e	t	h	o	y	i	u
n	e	s	q	h	e	a	d	r	t
l	u	k	w	f	a	r	u	t	s
i	d	e	i	o	r	m	e	s	d
s	k	l	n	o	t	z	y	k	e
o	m	e	d	t	s	b	e	i	w
h	e	t	p	b	r	a	i	n	i
t	c	o	i	q	b	l	o	o	d
s	a	n	p	d	o	w	b	l	s
w	i	m	e	p	n	i	t	u	a
m	u	s	c	l	e	c	l	n	e
s	t	o	m	a	c	h	a	g	n
e	r	a	y	n	k	o	r	s	h

Word Bank

head	arm	foot	brain	skeleton
bone	skin	blood	heart	windpipe
lungs	eye	muscle	teeth	stomach

What's for Lunch?

Name _____

We try to eat foods from each of the four food groups every day. Take a close look at your lunch today.

List each of the foods from your lunch in the correct food groups.

Fruits and Vegetables	Breads and Cereals
Dairy Foods	**Meats**

School Cafeteria

Alex and Maria are ready to choose their lunch in the school cafeteria. They know how important it is to eat a balanced meal.

Help them select foods from the four basic food groups. Write their food choices on the menus.

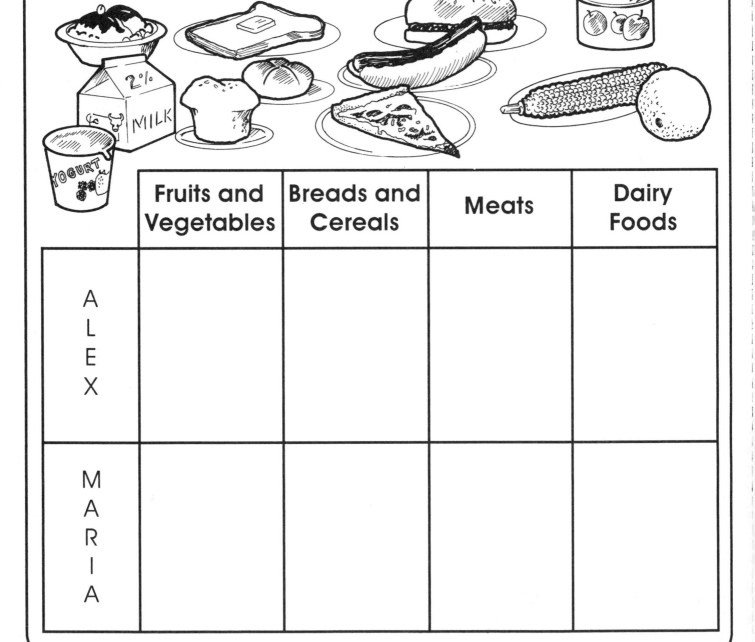

	Fruits and Vegetables	Breads and Cereals	Meats	Dairy Foods
A L E X				
M A R I A				

The Big Four

Name _____

It's important to eat foods from each of the four food groups every day.

Cut out the foods.

Paste them in the correct box.

Fruits and Vegetables	Breads and Cereals
Dairy Foods	**Meats**

Home Grain Inventory

Name _____

Many of the foods that we eat come from grains. Take a close look at the foods made from grain in your kitchen.

Write the name of the food. Check the grain it contains.	barley	corn	oats	rice	soybeans	wheat

Cloudy Weather

Clouds bring us many kinds of weather. Some clouds give us fair weather. Other clouds bring rain.

Paste the picture of the cloud next to its description.

	How the Clouds Look	Weather
	Big, puffy clouds	Nice day, but there might be a small shower.
	Tall, dark, piles of clouds.	Thunderstorm
	Whispy clouds that look like feathers.	Fair
	Layers of gray clouds that cover the whole sky.	Steady drizzle.

Stratus   Cumulus   Cumulo-nimbus   Cirrus

How Are Clouds Made?

Name _____

How are clouds made?
Cut out the pictures.
Paste them on the page to show the cycle.

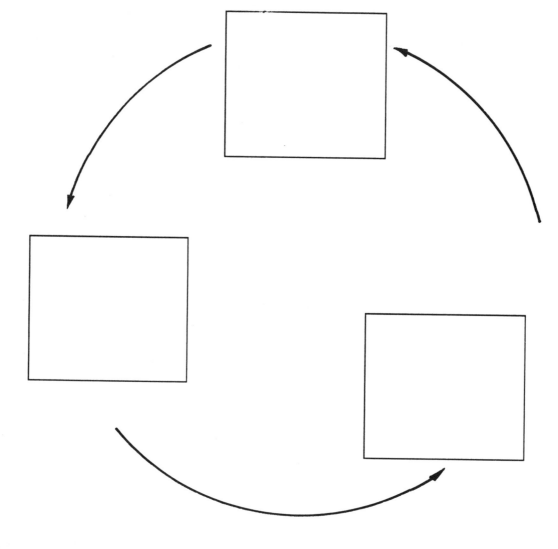

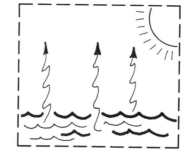
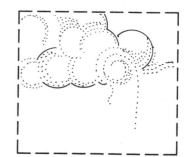

IF8757 Science Enrichment

The Water Cycle

Name _____

All of the water on earth travels on a never-ending journey. This journey is called the water cycle. There are three steps to the water cycle: **evaporation**, **condensation** and **precipitation**.

Write these steps where they belong on the picture below.

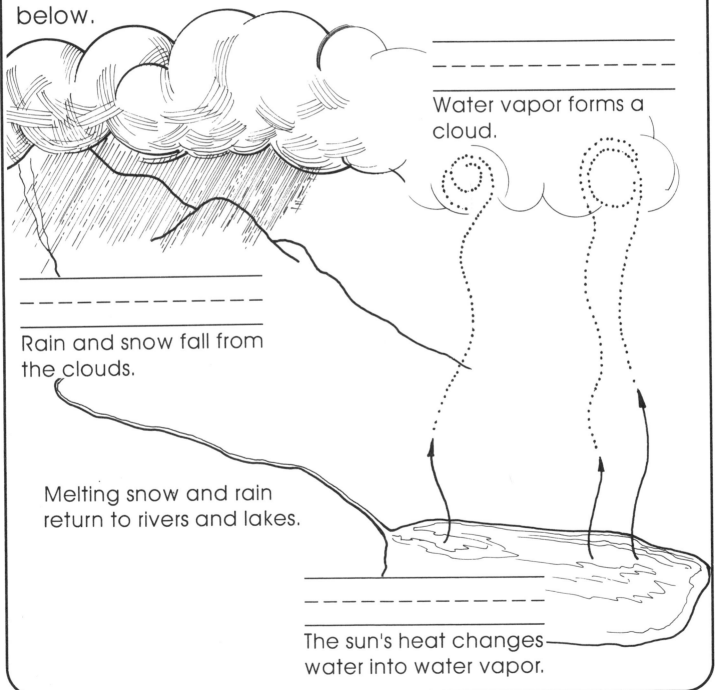

_____
- - - - - - - - - - - - - -

Water vapor forms a cloud.

_____
- - - - - - - - - - - - - -

Rain and snow fall from the clouds.

Melting snow and rain return to rivers and lakes.

_____
- - - - - - - - - - - - - -

The sun's heat changes water into water vapor.

Sky Watch

Name _____

Weather changes. Will tomorrow's weather be like today's? Keep a weather chart for one week.

Record the weather in the morning and afternoon by drawing the correct pictures on the chart below.

rain

snow

sunny

cloudy

partly cloudy

This Week's Weather				
	Monday	**Tuesday**	**Wednesday**	**Thursday**	**Friday**
A. M.					
P. M.					

A Nice Day Outside

Name _____

We like to play outside on hot days, cold days and mild days.

Look at the temperature in each picture.

Write the temperature and **hot, cold** or **mild** to tell what kind of day each is.

_ _ _ _ _ _ _ _ _ _ _ _

_____

_ _ _ _ _ _ _ _ _ _ _ _

_____

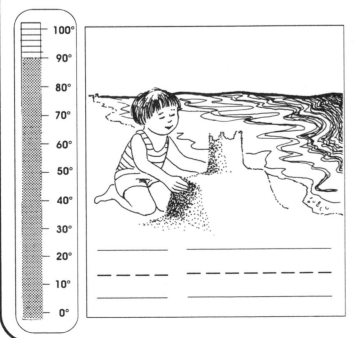

_____

_ _ _ _ _ _ _ _ _ _ _ _

_____

Hot or Cold?

Name _____

A thermometer tells us the temperature. Make your own thermometer and practice reading the temperature.

1. Color the bottom half of the tube red.

2. Cut out the tube.

3. Cut the slits **A** and **B** on the thermometer.

4. Fold and insert the ends of the tube in slits **A** and **B**.

5. Slide the tube up or down and read the different temperatures.

Fold back A

Slit A

- - - - -
——— 90°F
———
——— 80°
———
——— 70°
———
——— 60°
———
——— 50°
———
——— 40°
———
——— 30°
———
——— 20°
———
——— 10°
———
——— 0°
———
- - - - -

Slit B

tube →

Fold back B

Lifting with Levers

Name _____

A lever is a simple machine used to lift or move things. It has two parts. The **arm** is the part that moves. The **fulcrum** supports the arm and does not move.

Name the parts of this lever.

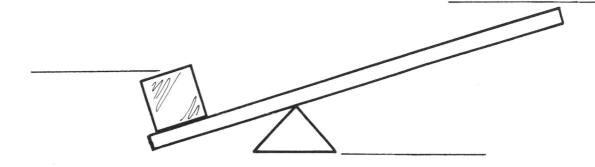

Unscramble the names of these levers.

velosh

_____
- - - - - - - - - -

mrahem

_____
- - - - - - - - - -

moorb

_____
- - - - - - - - - -

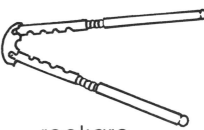

tun   reckarc

_____
- - - - - - - - - -
_____

Levers at Work

Name _____

Levers help make our work easier. Circle all the levers. Then find their names in the wordsearch.

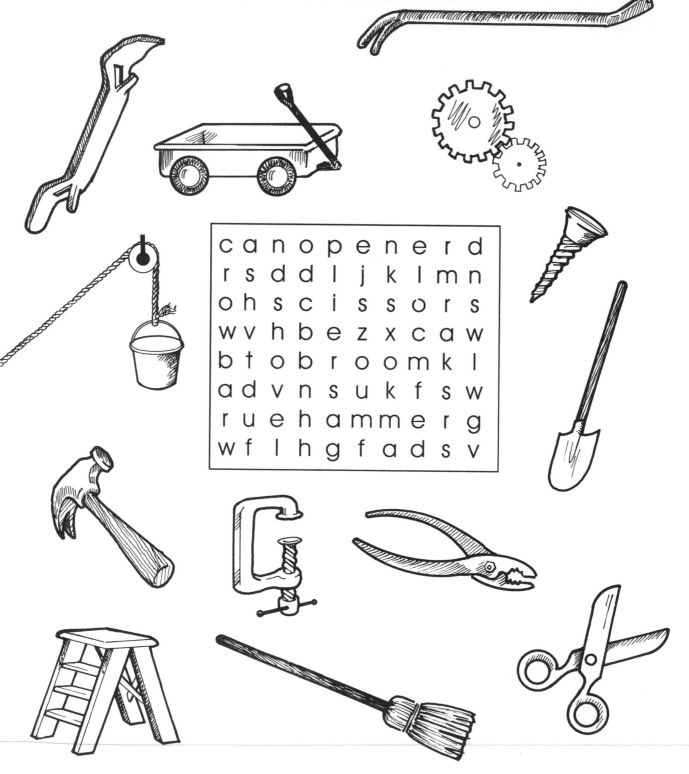

```
c a n o p e n e r d
r s d d l j k l m n
o h s c i s s o r s
w v h b e z x c a w
b t o b r o o m k l
a d v n s u k f s w
r u e h a m m e r g
w f l h g f a d s v
```

The Wedge

Name _____

A wedge is a type of inclined plane. It is made up of two inclined planes joined together to make a sharp edge. A wedge can be used to cut things. Some wedges are pointed.

Color only the pictures of wedges.

Machines with a Slant

Name _____

An inclined plane has a slanted surface. It is used to move things from a low place to a high place. Some inclined planes are smooth. Others have steps.

Color the inclined planes in the picture.

Screws

Name _____

A screw is a very helpful simple machine. It can be used to hold two pieces of wood together. It can not be pulled easily out of wood like a smooth nail.

1. Color part of the inclined plane as shown below.

2. Cut out the inclined plane.

3. Wrap it around a pencil as shown.

4. Tape it at the bottom.

5. Twirl the pencil with your fingers. What does it look like?

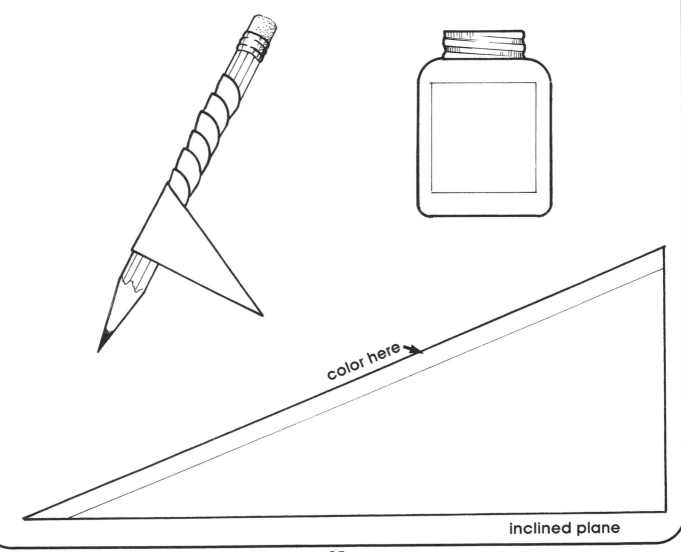

color here →

inclined plane

Six Simple Machines

Name _____

Welcome to *Simon's Simple Machine Shop*. Simon needs some help putting his simple machines where they belong. Color and cut out each simple machine. Glue each one in the correct place.

Simon's Simple Machine Shop

Screw	**Lever**	**Pulley**
Wedge	**Wheel and Axle**	**Inclined Plane**

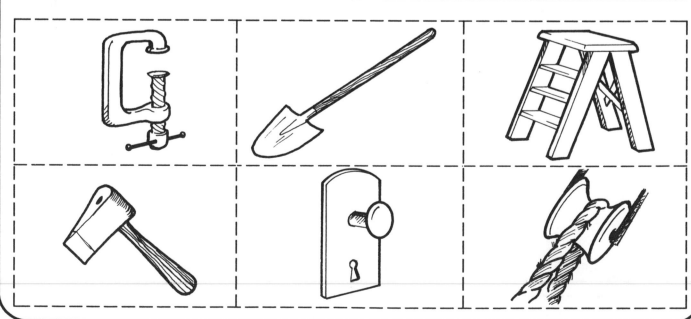

The Right Tool for the Job

Name _____

Mother gave Tyrone and Kim a list of jobs. Help them pick the right tool for each job. Draw a line from the job to the tool.

What will help Kim raise the flag up the flagpole?

inclined plane

What will Tyrone use to help him get the cat out of the tree.

pulley

What will Kim use to carry sand to her new sandbox?

lever

What will Tyrone use to get the nail out of the board?

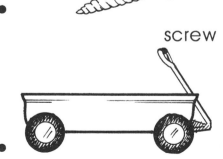
screw

What will Kim use to hang the mirror on her bedroom door?

wheel and axle

What will Tyrone use to slice the turkey?

wedge

IF8757 Science Enrichment

As Easy as 1 - 2 - 3!

Name _____

Machines make our work easier. There are many kinds of machines. Some machines are big and some are small. Some machines have many parts while some have just one.

Color and cut out the machines. Glue each one next to the picture that shows where it's needed on the Job Chart.

Job Chart

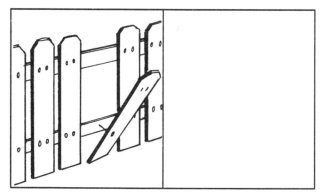

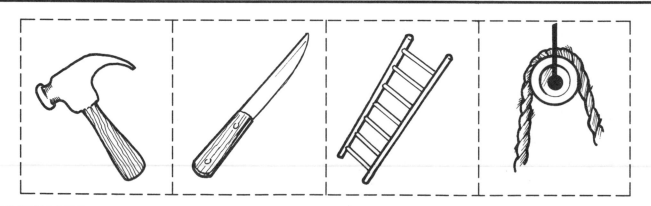

IF8757 Science Enrichment

Who Am I?

Name _____

Use the words in the Tool Box to name the simple machine in each picture. Then you will find the answer to this question.

What do machines use to do work? _____

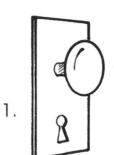
1.

2.

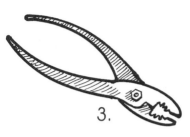
3.

1. ___ ___ ___ ___ □ ___ ___ ___ ___ ___ ___ ___ ___

2. ___ ___ ___ ___ ___ □ ___ ___ ___ ___ ___ ___ ___

3. ___ □ ___ ___ ___ ___

4. ___ ___ □ ___ ___ ___

4.

5. ___ ___ □ ___ ___ ___

6. ___ ___ ___ □ ___ ___ ___

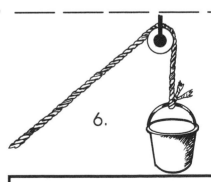
6.

5.

Tool Box		
wheel & axle	inclined plane	screw
wedge	lever	pulley

Magnets Pull

Name _____

Draw a line from the magnet to each thing that it can pull.

Push or Pull?

Name _____

Every magnet has a north pole and a south pole.

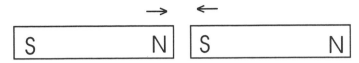

When a north pole and a south pole are next to each other they pull together.

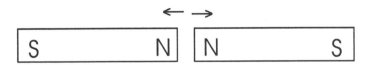

When two north poles, or two south poles are next to each other they push apart.

Tell what each pair of magnets will do below. Write **push** or **pull**.

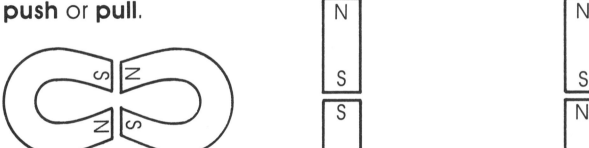

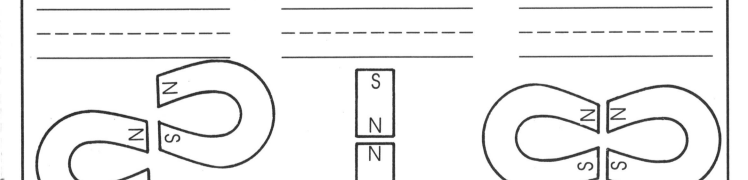

Sticky Hunt

Name _____

What things will a magnet stick to?

Make lists of the things in your room that will and will not stick to a magnet.

Magnets stick to:	Magnets do not stick to:

Caution: Do not try your magnet on these things.

TV	Computer disks
VCR	Cassette tapes
Computer	Video tapes
Radio	Credit cards
Tape recorder	Telephone

Answer Key

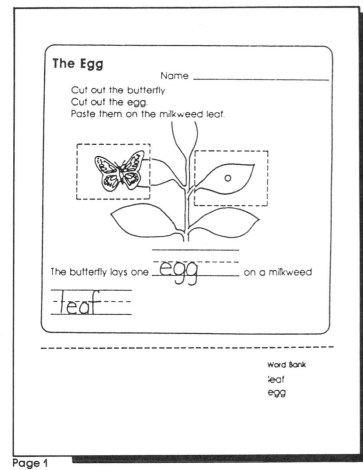

The Egg

Name _____

Cut out the butterfly
Cut out the egg.
Paste them on the milkweed leaf.

The butterfly lays one __egg__ on a milkweed __leaf__

Word Bank
leaf
egg

Page 1

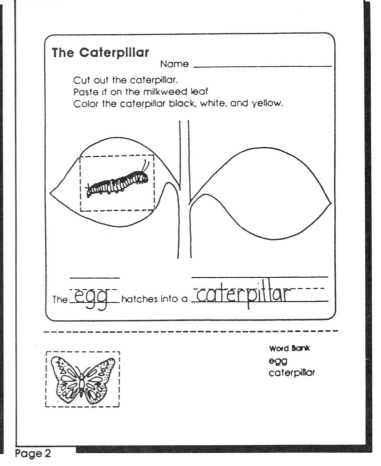

The Caterpillar

Name _____

Cut out the caterpillar.
Paste it on the milkweed leaf.
Color the caterpillar black, white, and yellow.

The __egg__ hatches into a __caterpillar__

Word Bank
egg
caterpillar

Page 2

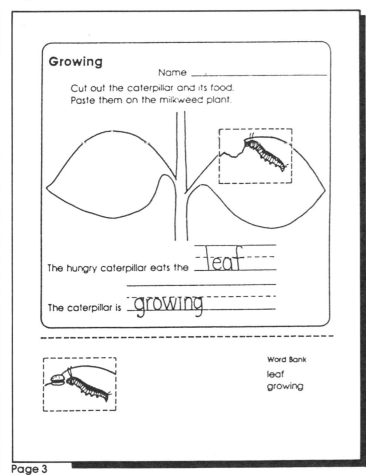

Growing

Name _____

Cut out the caterpillar and its food.
Paste them on the milkweed plant.

The hungry caterpillar eats the __leaf__

The caterpillar is __growing__

Word Bank
leaf
growing

Page 3

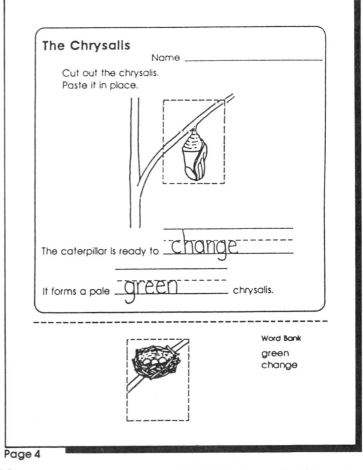

The Chrysalis

Name _____

Cut out the chrysalis.
Paste it in place.

The caterpillar is ready to __change__

It forms a pale __green__ chrysalis.

Word Bank
green
change

Page 4

Answer Key

The Butterfly

Name _____

Cut out the butterfly.
Paste it in place.

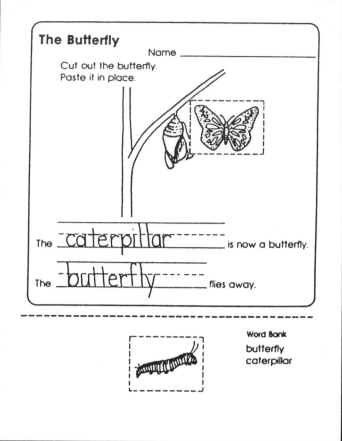

The ___caterpillar___ is now a butterfly.

The ___butterfly___ flies away.

- - - - - - - - - - - - - - - - - -

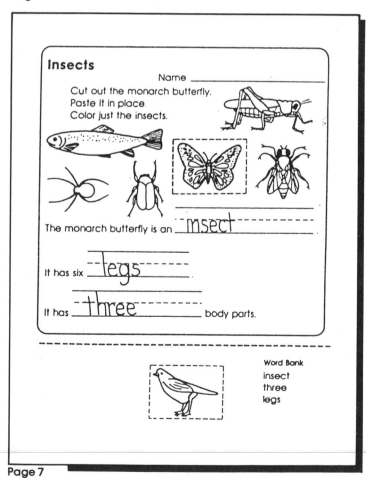

Word Bank
butterfly
caterpillar

Metamorphosis

Name _____

Show how the monarch changes.
Cut out the pictures.
Paste them in order.

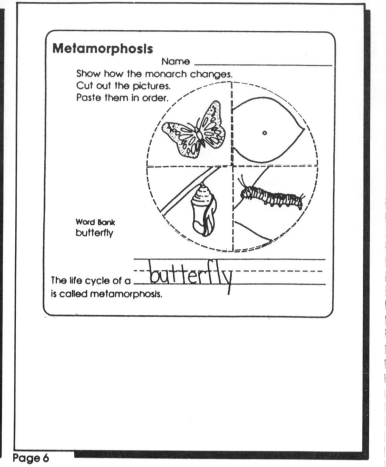

Word Bank
butterfly

The life cycle of a ___butterfly___
is called metamorphosis.

Insects

Name _____

Cut out the monarch butterfly.
Paste it in place.
Color just the insects.

The monarch butterfly is an ___insect___

It has six ___legs___

It has ___three___ body parts.

Word Bank
insect
three
legs

the Butterfly

by _____

IF8757 Science Enrichment

Answer Key

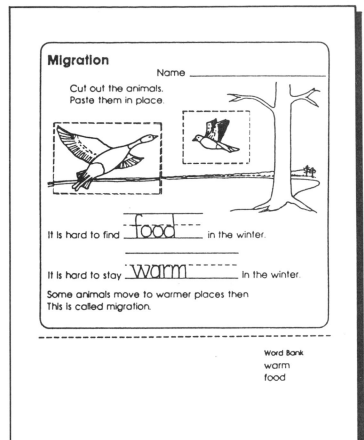

Migration

Name _____

Cut out the animals.
Paste them in place.

It is hard to find __food__ in the winter.

It is hard to stay __warm__ in the winter.

Some animals move to warmer places then
This is called migration.

Word Bank
warm
food

Page 9

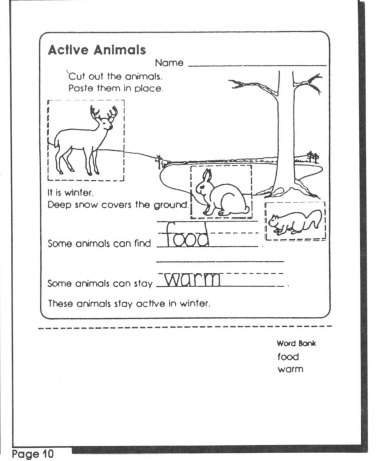

Active Animals

Name _____

Cut out the animals.
Paste them in place.

It is winter.
Deep snow covers the ground.

Some animals can find __food__

Some animals can stay __warm__.

These animals stay active in winter.

Word Bank
food
warm

Page 10

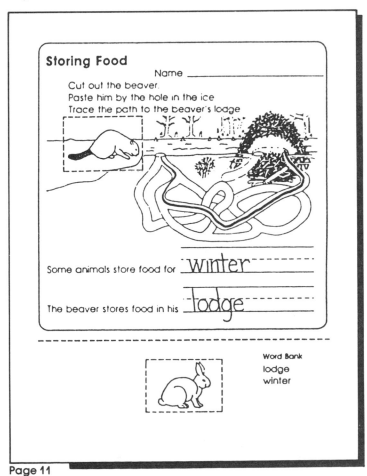

Storing Food

Name _____

Cut out the beaver.
Paste him by the hole in the ice
Trace the path to the beaver's lodge

Some animals store food for __winter__

The beaver stores food in his __lodge__

Word Bank
lodge
winter

Page 11

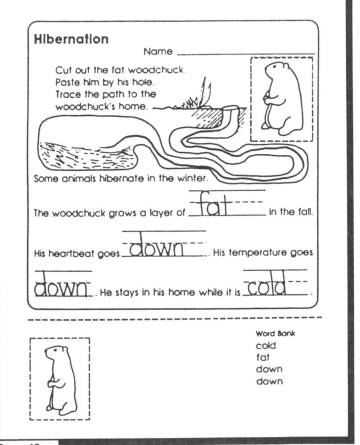

Hibernation

Name _____

Cut out the fat woodchuck.
Paste him by his hole.
Trace the path to the
woodchuck's home.

Some animals hibernate in the winter.

The woodchuck grows a layer of __fat__ in the fall.

His heartbeat goes __down__. His temperature goes

__down__. He stays in his home while it is __cold__

Word Bank
cold
fat
down
down

Page 12

Answer Key

Animals in Winter

Name _____

Cut out the animal.
Paste it in its place.
Write the animal's name.

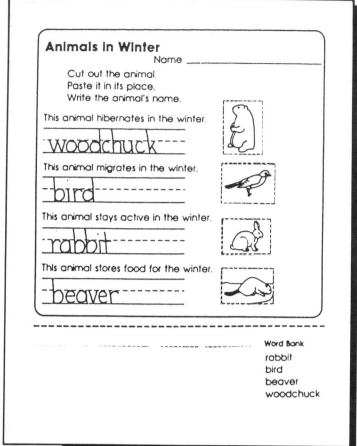

This animal hibernates in the winter.

woodchuck

This animal migrates in the winter.

bird

This animal stays active in the winter.

rabbit

This animal stores food for the winter.

beaver

_____   _____

Word Bank
rabbit
bird
beaver
woodchuck

Page 13

Page 14

Frogs

Name _____

Cut out the frogs.
Paste the big frog on the lily pad.
Paste the little frog on the log.
Trace the path from the log to the lily pad

Frogs can live in the **water**

Frogs can live on **land**

Frogs are amphibians.

Word Bank
land
water
frogs

Page 15

Laying Eggs

Name _____

Cut out the frog's eggs.
Paste them in the water.

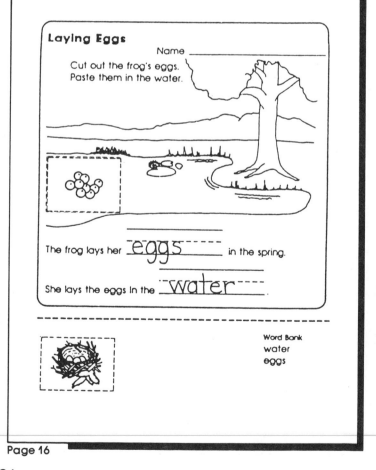

The frog lays her **eggs** in the spring.

She lays the eggs in the **water**

Word Bank
water
eggs

Page 16

106   IF8757 Science Enrichment

Tadpoles

Name _____

Cut out the tadpole.
Paste it in the water.

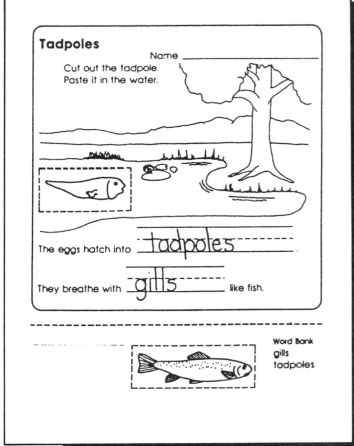

The eggs hatch into **tadpoles**.

They breathe with **gills** like fish.

Word Bank
gills
tadpoles

Growing

Name _____

Cut out the changing tadpole.
Paste it in the water.

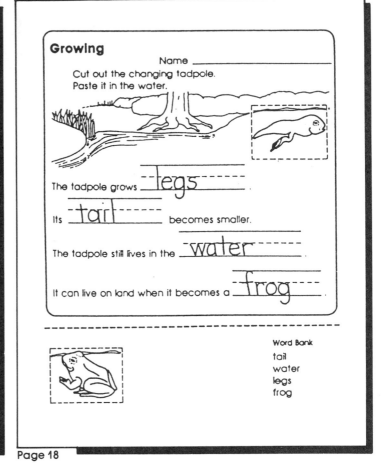

The tadpole grows **legs**.

Its **tail** becomes smaller.

The tadpole still lives in the **water**.

It can live on land when it becomes a **frog**.

Word Bank
tail
water
legs
frog

The Life Cycle of a Frog

Name _____

Cut out the pictures.
Paste them in order.
Write the name of each picture.

egg

frog

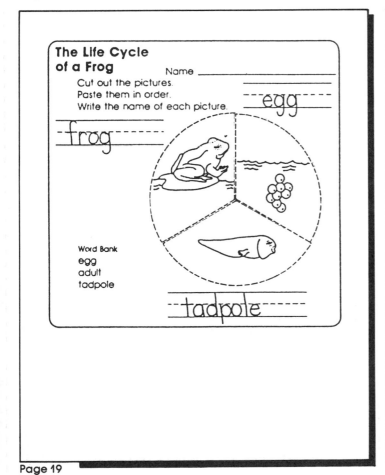

Word Bank
egg
adult
tadpole

tadpole

The Frog

by _____

Answer Key

Tree Parts

Name _____

Trees have three main parts. They are the trunk, the roots, and the leaves. Each part has a special job. Each part helps the tree.

Cut out the name of each part.
Cut out the job of each part.
Paste them on the picture.
Color the tree.

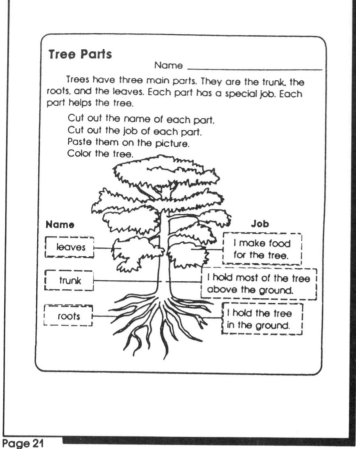

Name

leaves

trunk

roots

Job

I make food for the tree.

I hold most of the tree above the ground.

I hold the tree in the ground.

Leaf Shapes

Name _____

All leaves are not the same. They have different shapes. There are four common shapes.

Draw a line to match the leaf with its shape.

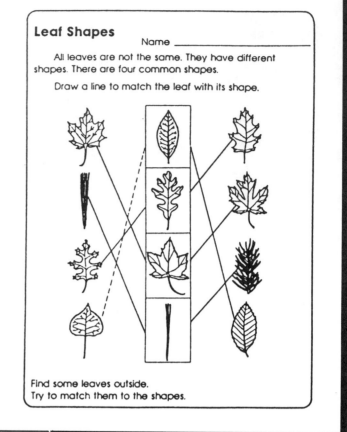

Find some leaves outside.
Try to match them to the shapes.

Leaf Study

Name _____

Put a leaf under the box on this paper. Rub the paper with the side of your crayon. Use the ruler at the bottom to measure your leaf.

This is a rubbing of my leaf.

Answers will vary.

1. The color of my leaf is _____.
2. My leaf is _____ cm wide and _____ cm long.
3. My leaf feels like _____
4. I found my leaf _____

cm 1   2   3   4   5   6   7   8   9

Food Factories

Name _____

Green leaves are like little factories. They make food for the tree. Leaves need sunshine, air, and water to make food.

Leaves change in the fall. They lose their green color. Then they cannot make food for the tree.

Draw a leaf.
This leaf can make food.
Color it green.
Write the correct word.

Draw another leaf.
This leaf cannot make food.
Color it with pretty fall colors.

green yellow

Food is made by *green* leaves.

shade sunshine

Leaves need *sunshine* to make food.

can cannot

Leaves *cannot* make food in the fall.

     IF8757 Science Enrichment

Answer Key

My Leaf Collection

Attach a leaf and fill in the blanks.

Teacher: Provide each student with three or more copies of this page so booklets can be made.

Tree _____
Location _____
Date _____

Page 25

Tree Seeds

Name _____

Some trees drop their seeds in the spring. Other trees drop their seeds in the fall. The seeds grow up. Do you know what they grow up to be?

Show how the acorn grows into a mighty oak tree. Write first, second, or third under the pictures to put them in order. Color the pictures.

first   third   second

Finish the story.
I am a little acorn. One day _____
_____
_____
_____
_____

Page 26

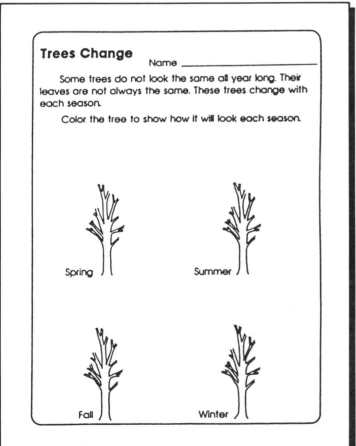

Trees Change

Name _____

Some trees do not look the same all year long. Their leaves are not always the same. These trees change with each season.

Color the tree to show how it will look each season.

Spring   Summer

Fall   Winter

Page 27

Trees Are Different

Name _____

Some trees change with the seasons. Other trees do not change with the seasons. They stay green all year long. These trees are called evergreens.

Color the trees to show how they are different each season.

Spring   Summer

Fall   Winter

Page 28

Answer Key

Trees Give Us Food

Name _____

People can eat the food from trees. Animals can also eat the food from trees. The food comes from different parts of the tree.

Label the foods that people get from trees.

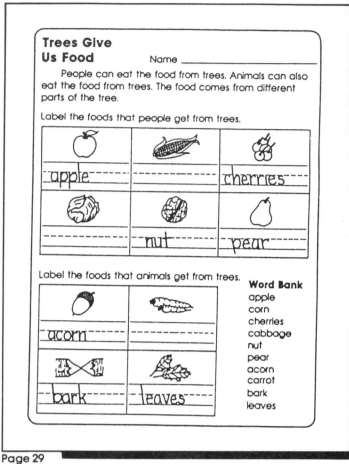

apple | | cherries
| |
| nut | pear

Label the foods that animals get from trees.

acorn |
|
bark | leaves

Word Bank
apple
corn
cherries
cabbage
nut
pear
acorn
carrot
bark
leaves

Page 29

I'm a Tree

Name _____

Write the answer to each riddle in the puzzle.

Across
4. I'm left over after a fire.
5. Part of me can be used to make bouncing balls.
6. My fruit is very sour.
7. I am either green or black.
8. George Washington chopped me down.

Down
1. I make great syrup.
2. Many drink my fruit's juice for breakfast.
3. Some say I keep the doctor away.

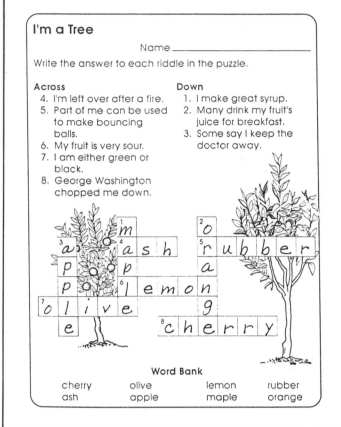

Word Bank

cherry   olive   lemon   rubber
ash   apple   maple   orange

Page 30

Trees Help Us

Name _____

Trees are used in many ways. Sometimes we eat the food from trees. Sometimes we build things with the wood from trees. Can you name some tree products?

Draw a line from the tree products to the tree. Circle the tree products.

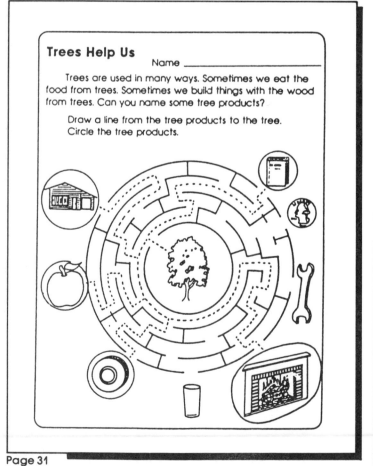

Page 31

Sugar Bush

Name _____

Spring is maple syrup time. People collect the sap from maple trees. They boil the sap until it becomes maple syrup. It takes thirty gallons of sap to make one gallon of syrup.

Color the pictures.
Write numbers next to the pictures in the order that maple syrup is made.

Page 32

          IF8757 Science Enrichment

Answer Key

Many Kinds of Trees
Name _____

There are many kinds of trees. Each kind has a different name. Can you name some trees?

Circle the hidden trees.

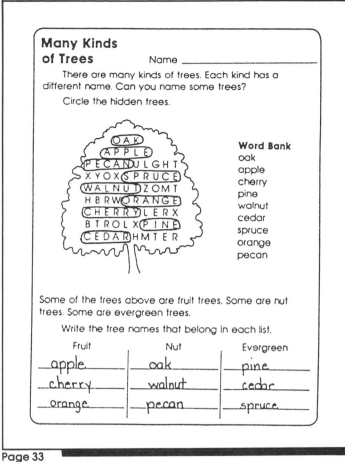

Word Bank
oak
apple
cherry
pine
walnut
cedar
spruce
orange
pecan

Some of the trees above are fruit trees. Some are nut trees. Some are evergreen trees.

Write the tree names that belong in each list.

Fruit	Nut	Evergreen
apple	oak	pine
cherry	walnut	cedar
orange	pecan	spruce

Plant Parts
Name _____

A plant has many parts. Each part has a special job.

Word Bank   roots   stem
        flower   leaf

Label the parts of the plant.

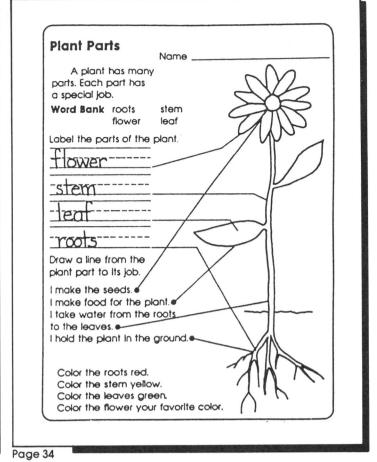

flower
stem
leaf
roots

Draw a line from the plant part to its job.

I make the seeds.
I make food for the plant.
I take water from the roots to the leaves.
I hold the plant in the ground.

Color the roots red.
Color the stem yellow.
Color the leaves green.
Color the flower your favorite color.

We Eat Plants
Name _____

We eat many foods. Some foods come from animals. Some foods come from plants.

Label the foods we get from plants.
Color the foods we get from plants.

Word Bank
banana   carrot
bread   cabbage
apple   corn

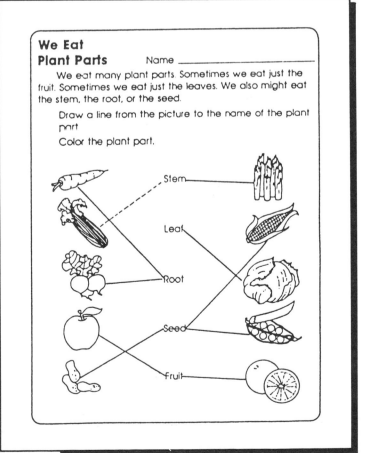

apple   bread

corn   banana

carrot   cabbage

We Eat Plant Parts
Name _____

We eat many plant parts. Sometimes we eat just the fruit. Sometimes we eat just the leaves. We also might eat the stem, the root, or the seed.

Draw a line from the picture to the name of the plant part

Color the plant part.

Stem
Leaf
Root
Seed
Fruit

IF8757 Science Enrichment

Answer Key

Growing Plants

Name _____

Color the pictures.
Cut them out.
Staple the pictures together.
Put the pictures in order on top of each other.
The youngest plant should be on the top.
Flip the pages and watch the plant grow.

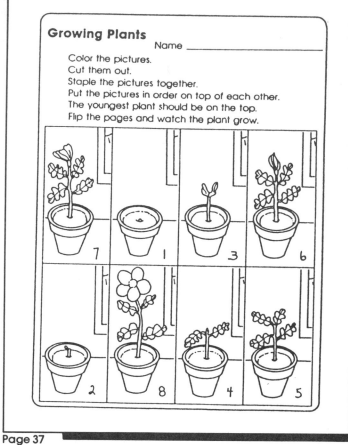

Plants Need Sunshine

Name _____

Mr. Right and Mr. Wrong planted gardens. Mr. Right planted his garden in the sun. Mr. Wrong planted his garden in the shade. Both of them gave their gardens love and care.

Draw what Mr. Right's garden will look like.

Draw what Mr. Wrong's garden will look like.

Plants Need Water

Name _____

Mrs. Right planted her flower seeds last week. She planted them in the sun. She gave her flowers water.

Mrs. Wrong planted her flower seeds last week. She planted them in the sun. But she forgot to give them water.

Draw what Mrs. Right's flowers will look like.

Draw what Mrs. Wrong's flowers will look like.

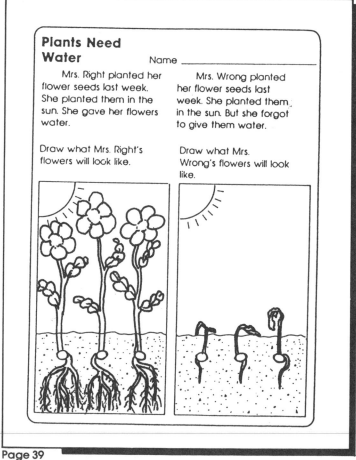

Plants Have Seeds

Name _____

Seeds are found in different parts of the plant. Some seeds are found in the flower. Some seeds are found in the fruit or the nut.

Circle the part of the plant that has the seed. Write the name of the seed.

Word Bank
pine
apple
corn
maple
acorn
dandelion

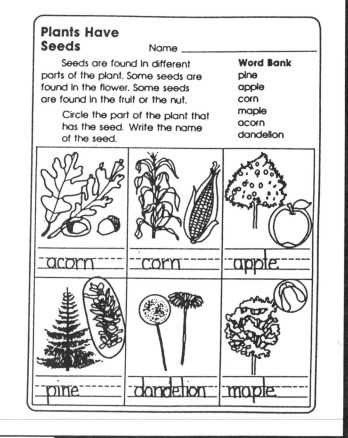

acorn | corn | apple

pine | dandelion | maple

IF8757 Science Enrichment

Answer Key

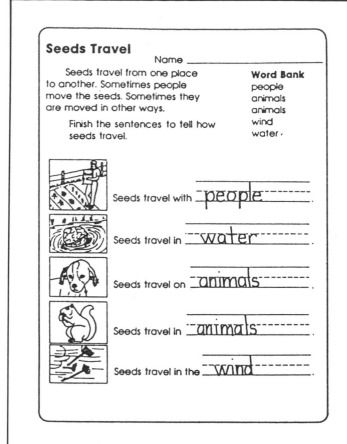

Seeds Travel

Name _____

Seeds travel from one place to another. Sometimes people move the seeds. Sometimes they are moved in other ways.

Finish the sentences to tell how seeds travel.

Word Bank
people
animals
animals
wind
water

Seeds travel with _people_ .

Seeds travel in _water_ .

Seeds travel on _animals_ .

Seeds travel in _animals_ .

Seeds travel in the _wind_ .

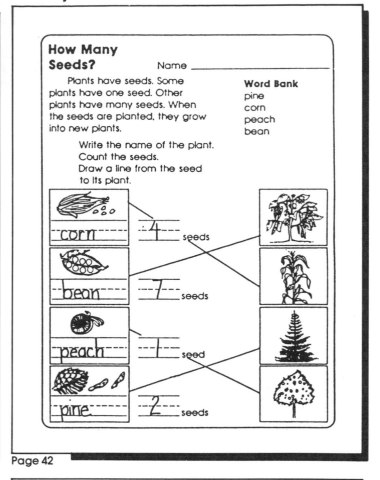

How Many Seeds?

Name _____

Plants have seeds. Some plants have one seed. Other plants have many seeds. When the seeds are planted, they grow into new plants.

Word Bank
pine
corn
peach
bean

Write the name of the plant.
Count the seeds.
Draw a line from the seed to its plant.

corn _4_ seeds

bean _7_ seeds

peach _1_ seed

pine _2_ seeds

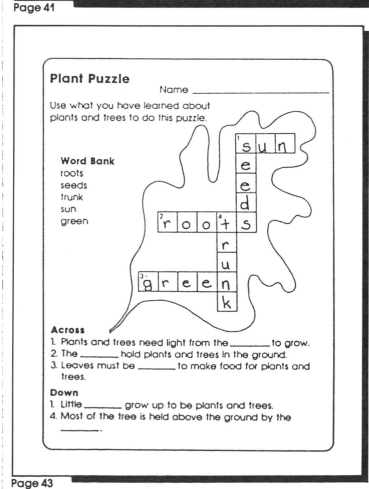

Plant Puzzle

Name _____

Use what you have learned about plants and trees to do this puzzle.

Word Bank
roots
seeds
trunk
sun
green

```
        s u n
        e
        e
    r o o t s
        r
        u
  g r e e n
        k
```

Across
1. Plants and trees need light from the _____ to grow.
2. The _____ hold plants and trees in the ground.
3. Leaves must be _____ to make food for plants and trees.

Down
1. Little _____ grow up to be plants and trees.
4. Most of the tree is held above the ground by the _____ .

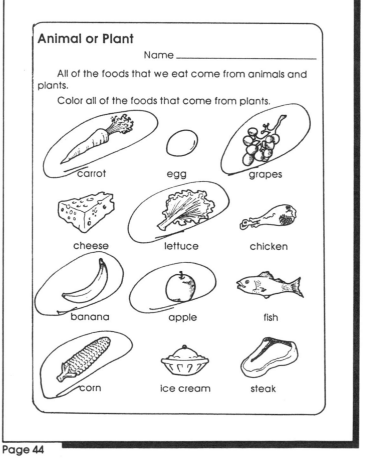

Animal or Plant

Name _____

All of the foods that we eat come from animals and plants.

Color all of the foods that come from plants.

carrot   egg   grapes

cheese   lettuce   chicken

banana   apple   fish

corn   ice cream   steak

Answer Key

All in the Family

Name _____

Put an **X** on the animal that does not belong.

1.
2.
3.
4.
5.

I'm Bigger than You

Name _____

Color the pictures and cut them out.

Glue them in order on a sheet of paper from smallest to largest.

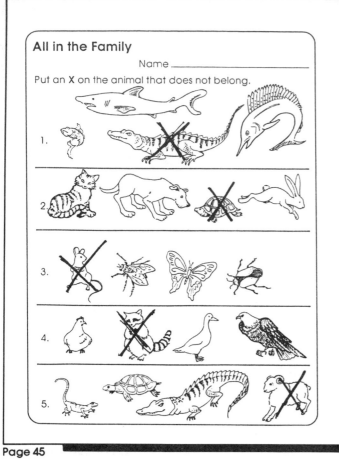

3   4
6   2
5   1

Animals on the Go!

Name _____

How do these animals move?

Write **walk**, **fly** or **swim**.

swim   *walk*   *fly*

swim   *walk*   *fly*

fly   *walk*   *swim*

At Home in the Pond Community

Name _____

Many animals make their homes in a pond community, but some of the animals in this picture do not belong.

Draw an **X** on the animals that do **not** belong.

       IF8757 Science Enrichment

Answer Key

At Home in the Grassland Community

Name _____

Many animals make their homes in a grassland community, but some of the animals in this picture do not belong.

Draw an **X** on the animals that do **not** belong.

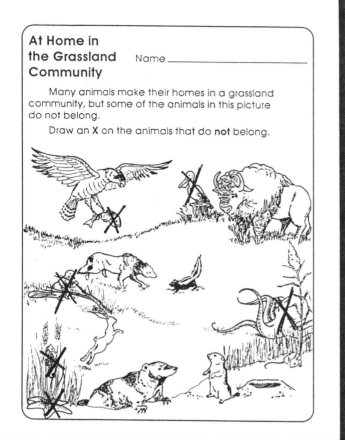

At Home in the Ocean Community

Name _____

Many animals make their homes in an ocean community, but some of the animals in this picture do not belong.

Draw an **X** on the animals that do **not** belong.

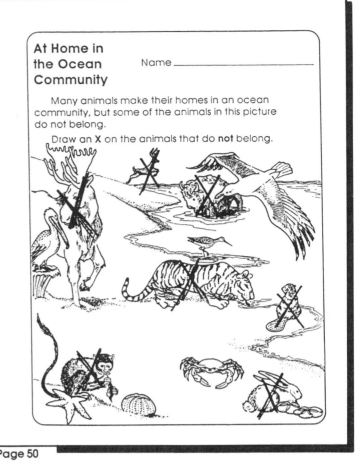

At Home in the Forest Community

Name _____

Many animals make their homes in a forest community, but some of the animals in this picture do not belong.

Draw an **X** on the animals that do **not** belong.

Animals at Home

Name _____

Did you ever see a fish living in a tree? Of course you didn't! Fish live in the water. Help the animals find their homes.

Cut out each animal. Paste it on its home. Color the picture.

IF8757 Science Enrichment

Answer Key

Young Animals

Name _____

Many young animals look like their parents. But some do not look like their parents.

Draw a line from the parent to its young.

Write the name of the young.

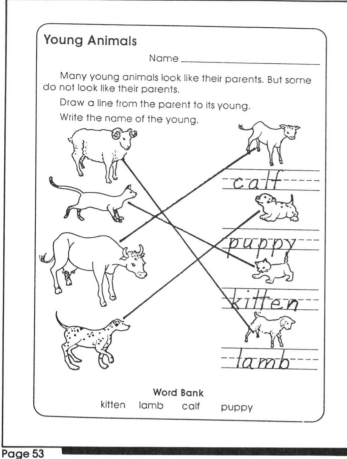

Word Bank

kitten   lamb   calf   puppy

Page 53

Food Chain

Name _____

The living things on this page are all part of a food chain. A food chain is the order in which living things get their energy. This food chain begins with energy from the sun.

Cut out the living things.

Paste them in order on the food chain.

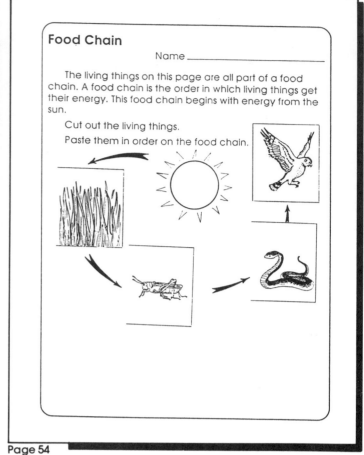

Page 54

Links in a Chain

Name _____

There are many kinds of living things on this page. You can make a model food chain using the pictures.

1. Color the pictures below and cut them out.
2. Glue each picture to a 2-x-10-inch strip of paper.
3. Make a chain with the strips of paper in the order of a food chain.

Page 55

Animal Boxes

Name *Answers may vary.*

In each box, write the name of two animals that fit the description.

butterfly bee beetle insect	snail robin fish lizard turtle hawk turkey lays eggs	fish whale seal snail clam has no legs	turkey robin hawk has feathers
snail clam fish whale turtle seal lives in water	horse goat turkey pig cow farm animal	snail clam turtle beetle has a hard shell	butterfly turkey bat bee hawk robin beetle has wings
horse deer giraffe lion runs fast	deer moose goat has horns or antlers	fish lizard has scales	snail cow turtle clam very slow
whale elephant cow moose horse pig very strong	goat cow giraffe horse moose cat lion has hair	giraffe moose horse elephant deer goat has long legs	horse cat turtle cow lizard pig fish is a good pet

giraffe snail fish turtle	butterfly elephant turkey bee pig	cow robin deer goat lizard	horse beetle seal moose whale	clam cat bat lion hawk

Page 56

116

IF8757 Science Enrichment

Answer Key

My Bird List

Name _____

Bird watchers keep a list of all the different kinds of birds they have seen. They also keep track of the date and location. Begin a list of your own using the chart below.

Bird	Date	Location
Answers will vary.		

Feathered Friends

Name _____

Name the parts of the bird.

feathers — *bill* — *wings* — *feet*

Read the riddle. Name each bird part.

I keep a bird warm and dry. What am I? *feathers*
I help a bird stand or swim. What am I? *feet*
I help a bird eat. What am I? *bill*
I make a bird fly high in the sky. What am I? *wings*

Word Bank			
feathers	feet	bill	wings

Birds

Name _____

Do the puzzle about birds.
Color only the birds.

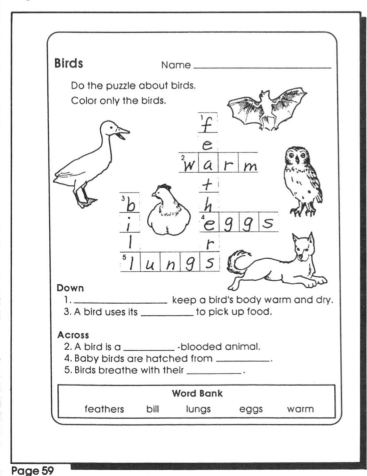

Crossword answers:
1. f e a t h e r
2. w a r m
3. b i l l
4. e g g s
5. l u n g s

Down
1. _____ keep a bird's body warm and dry.
3. A bird uses its _____ to pick up food.

Across
2. A bird is a _____ -blooded animal.
4. Baby birds are hatched from _____.
5. Birds breathe with their _____.

Word Bank				
feathers	bill	lungs	eggs	warm

Reptiles

Name _____

Do the puzzle about reptiles.
Color only the reptiles.

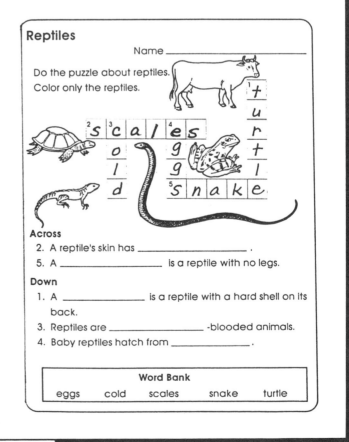

Crossword answers:
1. t u r t l e
2. s c a l e s
3. c o l d
4. e g g
5. s n a k e

Across
2. A reptile's skin has _____.
5. A _____ is a reptile with no legs.

Down
1. A _____ is a reptile with a hard shell on its back.
3. Reptiles are _____ -blooded animals.
4. Baby reptiles hatch from _____.

Word Bank				
eggs	cold	scales	snake	turtle

         IF8757 Science Enrichment

Answer Key

Amphibians

Name _____

Do the puzzle about amphibians.
Color only the amphibians.

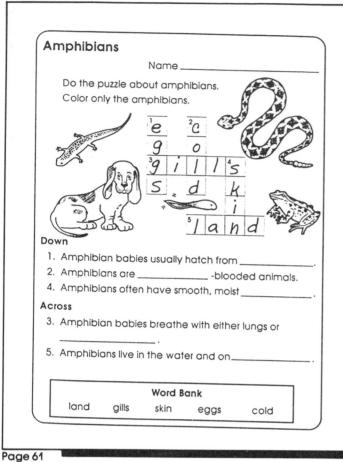

```
¹e  ²c
 g   o
³g i l l ⁴s
 s     . k
      ²  i
   ⁵l a n d
```

Down

1. Amphibian babies usually hatch from _____.
2. Amphibians are _____ -blooded animals.
4. Amphibians often have smooth, moist _____.

Across

3. Amphibian babies breathe with either lungs or
   _____.

5. Amphibians live in the water and on_____.

Word Bank				
land	gills	skin	eggs	cold

Page 61

Mammals

Name _____

Do the puzzle about mammals.
Color only the mammals.

```
        ¹w
²h a i r
    r
³m i l k
    u
    n
    g
⁵b a b i e s
```

Down

1. Mammals are _____ -blooded.
4. Mammals breathe with _____ .

Across

2. A mammal's body is usually covered with _____.
3. Mother mammals feed _____ to their babies.
5. Mammal's _____ are born alive.

Word Bank				
hair	babies	lungs	milk	warm

Page 62

Fish

Name _____

Do the puzzle about fish.
Color only the fish.

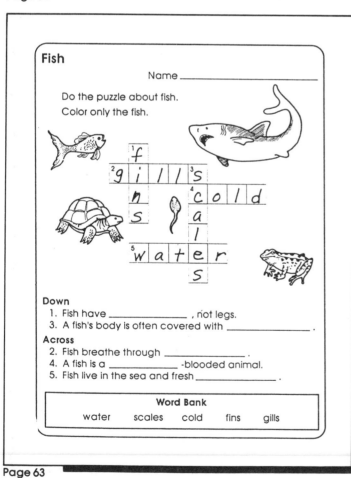

```
   ¹f
²g i l l ³s
   n   ⁴c o l d
   s    a
        l
   ⁵w a t e r
        s
```

Down

1. Fish have _____ , not legs.
3. A fish's body is often covered with _____.

Across

2. Fish breathe through _____ .
4. A fish is a _____ -blooded animal.
5. Fish live in the sea and fresh _____ .

Word Bank				
water	scales	cold	fins	gills

Page 63

Insects

Name _____

Do the puzzle about insects.
Color only the insects.

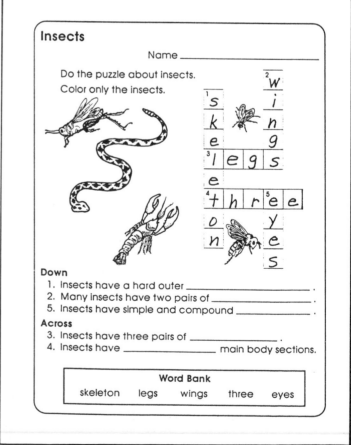

```
              ²w
  ¹s          i
   k          n
  ³l e g s
   e
  ⁴t h r e ⁵e
   o        y
   n        e
            s
```

Down

1. Insects have a hard outer _____.
2. Many insects have two pairs of _____.
5. Insects have simple and compound _____.

Across

3. Insects have three pairs of _____.
4. Insects have _____ main body sections.

Word Bank				
skeleton	legs	wings	three	eyes

Page 64

Answer Key

Bones Give You Shape

Name _____

Bones give your body shape. They let you stand up tall. You cannot see your bones. But you can feel many of your bones under your skin

Draw a line from each bone to the part of the body where it is found. Write the name of the bone(s).

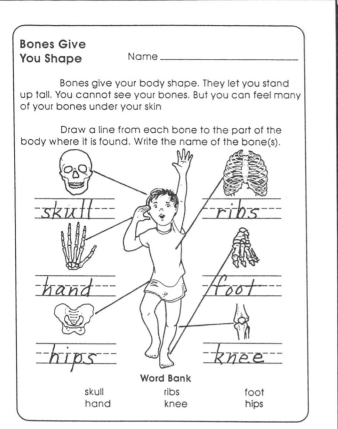

skull

ribs

hand

foot

hips

knee

Word Bank

skull	ribs	foot
hand	knee	hips

Name That Bone

Name _____

Name these bones of your skeleton.

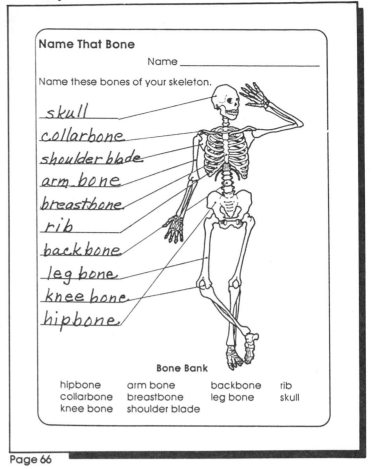

skull
collarbone
shoulder blade
arm bone
breastbone
rib
backbone
leg bone
knee bone
hipbone

Bone Bank

hipbone	arm bone	backbone	rib
collarbone	breastbone	leg bone	skull
knee bone	shoulder blade		

Mr. Bones
(Use with page 68.)

Name _____

Hi, my name is Mr. Bones. This is my skeleton. It gives me my shape. It helps my body move. It also protects my heart, lungs and brain from injury.

1. Cut out my bones.
2. Put them together with brads, matching the letters, A to A, etc.

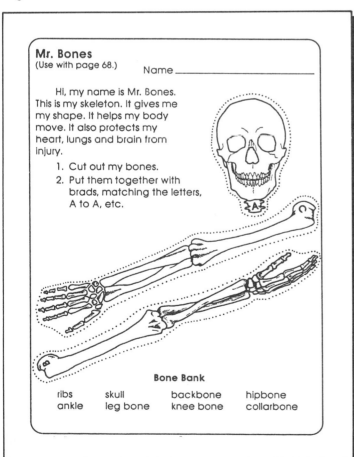

Bone Bank

ribs	skull	backbone	hipbone
ankle	leg bone	knee bone	collarbone

Mr. Bones
(Continued)

Name _____

Use with page 67.

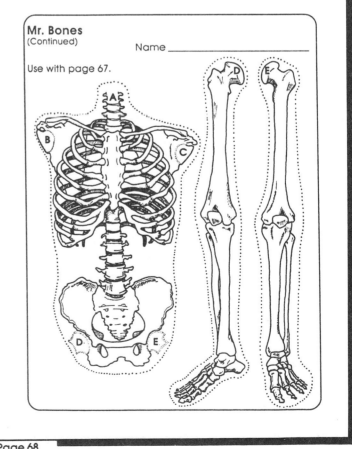

Answer Key

Crossbones

Name _____

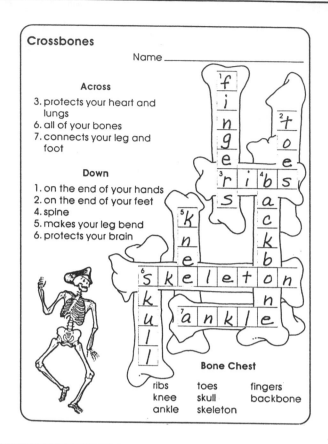

Across

3. protects your heart and lungs
6. all of your bones
7. connects your leg and foot

Down

1. on the end of your hands
2. on the end of your feet
4. spine
5. makes your leg bend
6. protects your brain

Crossword answers:
- 1 down: finger
- 2 down: toes
- 3 across: ribs
- 4 down: backbone
- 5 down: knee
- 5 down: skull
- 6 across: skeleton
- 7 across: ankle

Bone Chest

ribs	toes	fingers
knee	skull	backbone
ankle	skeleton	

Eating Good Food

Name _____

The food you eat takes a long trip through your body through your digestive system. Foods are broken down during the journey. The nutrients from the food give your body energy to work and grow.

Color the parts of your digestive system.

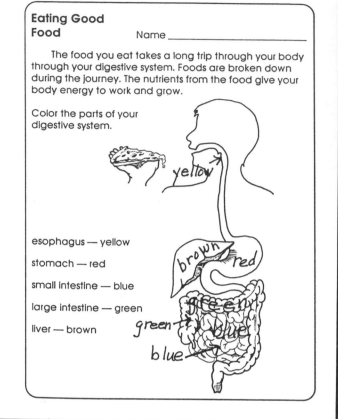

yellow

brown   red

green

blue

esophagus — yellow

stomach — red

small intestine — blue

large intestine — green

liver — brown

Inside Me
(Part 1)   Name _____

If you could look under your skin, what would you find? You would find muscles, bones, a heart, a brain and many other body parts. Make a model of your insides to show where many of these parts are found.

You will need a friend to help you with the first step of your project.

1. Lay on your back on a large sheet of butcher paper. Turn your head so you are looking over your left shoulder.

2. Have your friend trace your outline with a pencil.

3. Use a dark crayon or marker and trace boldly over the penciled outline.

4. Follow the directions on the following pages.

Optional: You may cut out two body shapes. Glue the body parts on one shape. Staple the other shape underneath it, leaving an opening. Stuff the body with crumpled newspaper to make a 3-D model of you. Finish stapling.

Inside Me—My Brain
(Part 2)   Name _____

My brain has a very important job. It must keep my body working day and night. My brain has three parts.

The **cerebrum** is the largest part of my brain. It does my thinking.

The **cerebellum** makes my muscles move smoothly.

The **brain stem** controls my breathing and the beating of my heart.

1. Color the brain gray.
2. Cut out the brain
3. Glue the brain to your paper body.

cerebrum

cerebellum   brainstem

IF8757 Science Enrichment

Answer Key

Inside Me—Stomach

(Part 3)   Name _____

My stomach is a kind of bag. It can hold about two pints of food. Food travels from my mouth to my stomach through a long tube, called the esophagus. Stomach juices mix with food to help digestion.

My stomach is found on the left side of my body. It is protected by my five lower ribs.

1. Color your stomach blue.
2. Cut out your stomach and glue it to your paper body.
3. Draw a food tube (esophagus) from your stomach to your mouth. Color the food tube brown.

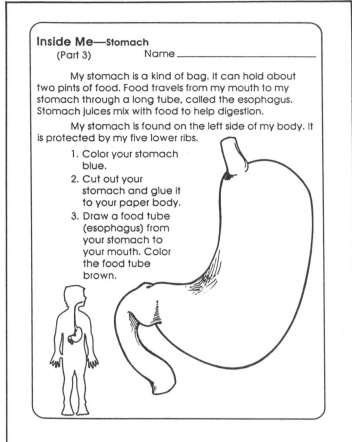

Inside Me—Intestines

(Part 4)   Name _____

Food is broken down in my small intestine. The nutrients are carried away by the blood in millions of small tubes. The leftover waste goes through my large intestine and out my body.

blue

orange

1. Color the small intestine orange and the large intestine blue.
2. Glue the intestines to your paper body. Connect the small intestine to the stomach.

Inside Me—Heart

(Part 5)   Name _____

My heart is a very strong pump. It pumps blood through more than 80,000 miles of tubes (arteries and veins) in my body. My heart is not very big. It is about the size of my fist and weighs less than one pound.

1. Color the heart red.
2. Cut out the heart. Fold and glue the tabs to your paper body.

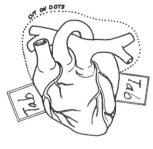

CUT ON DOTS

Tab   Tab

Inside Me—Lungs

(Part 6)   Name _____

My lungs take in the air that I breathe and give it to my blood. My blood takes it to all the cells in my body.

1. Color the windpipe and bronchus blue and the lungs red on pages 76 and 77.
2. Cut out the lungs on both pages.
3. Glue the left lung to the right lung on Tab A.
4. Bend and glue both Tabs B to the paper body. (Glue only the tabs.)
5. Draw a windpipe from the lungs to the mouth.

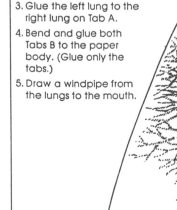

A

B

121   IF8757 Science Enrichment

Answer Key

Inside Me—Lungs
(Part 6 - continued)
Name _____

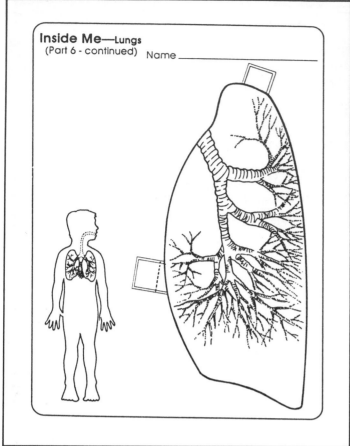

Page 77

Inside Me—Bones
(Part 7)
Name _____

My bones are very important. My leg bones and arm bones help me move. My skull and ribs protect the soft organs inside my body. Some of my bones make new blood cells for my body.

1. Color the bones yellow.
2. Glue them to your right arm.

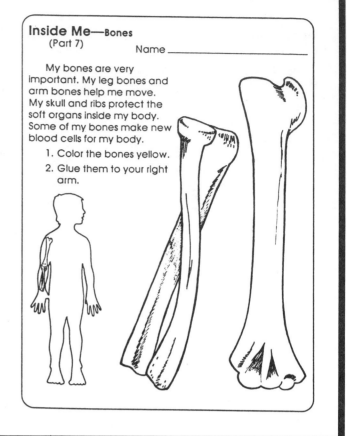

Page 78

Inside Me—Muscles
(Part 8)
Name _____

My muscles make my body move. They are connected to my bones with tendons. One muscle helps my arm bend and the other one helps to straighten it out.

1. Color the muscles red.
2. Cut out and glue the muscles to the bones on the right arm.

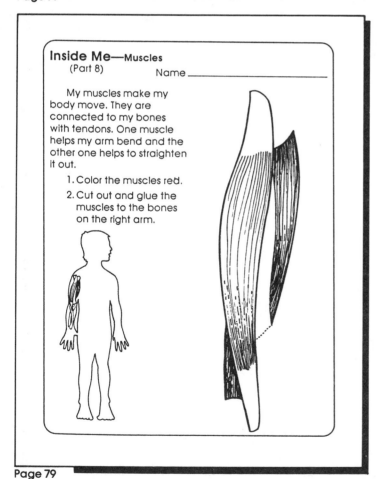

Page 79

Body Language
Name _____

Circle the words that are part of your body.

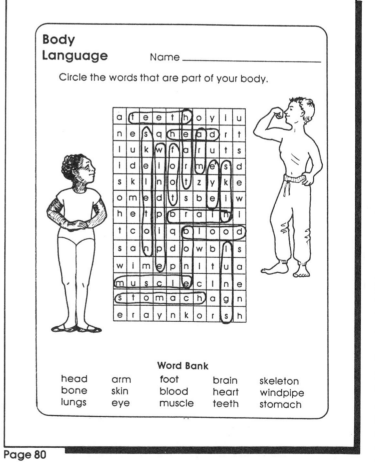

Word Bank

head	arm	foot	brain	skeleton
bone	skin	blood	heart	windpipe
lungs	eye	muscle	teeth	stomach

Page 80

Answer Key

What's for Lunch?

Name _____

We try to eat foods from each of the four food groups every day. Take a close look at your lunch today.

List each of the foods from your lunch in the correct food groups.

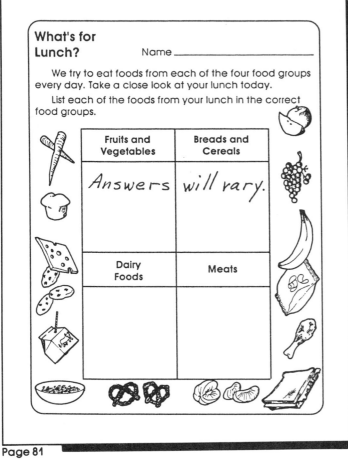

Fruits and Vegetables	Breads and Cereals
Answers	will vary.
Dairy Foods	**Meats**

Page 81

School Cafeteria

Name _____

Alex and Maria are ready to choose their lunch in the school cafeteria. They know how important it is to eat a balanced meal.

Help them select foods from the four basic food groups. Write their food choices on the menus.

	Fruits and Vegetables	Breads and Cereals	Meats	Dairy Foods
A L E X	Answers will vary.			
M A R I A				

Page 82

The Big Four

Name _____

It's important to eat foods from each of the four food groups every day.

Cut out the foods.

Paste them in the correct box.

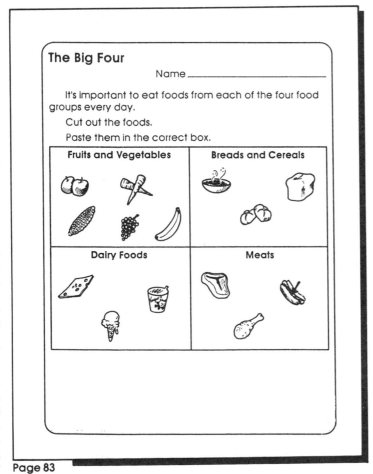

Fruits and Vegetables	Breads and Cereals
Dairy Foods	**Meats**

Page 83

Home Grain Inventory

Name _____

Many of the foods that we eat come from grains. Take a close look at the foods made from grain in your kitchen.

Write the name of the food. Check the grain it contains.	barley	corn	oats	rice	soybeans	wheat
Answers will vary.						

Page 84

Answer Key

Cloudy Weather

Name_____

Clouds bring us many kinds of weather. Some clouds give us fair weather. Other clouds bring rain.

Paste the picture of the cloud next to its description.

	How the Clouds Look	Weather
Cumulus	Big, puffy clouds	Nice day, but there might be a small shower.
Cumulo-nimbus	Tall, dark, piles of clouds.	Thunderstorm
Cirrus	Whispy clouds that look like feathers.	Fair
Stratus	Layers of gray clouds that cover the whole sky.	Steady drizzle.

How Are Clouds Made?

Name_____

How are clouds made?
Cut out the pictures.
Paste them on the page to show the cycle.

The Water Cycle

Name_____

All of the water on earth travels on a never-ending journey. This journey is called the water cycle. There are three steps to the water cycle: **evaporation**, **condensation** and **precipitation**.

Write these steps where they belong on the picture below.

condensation
Water vapor forms a cloud.

precipitation
Rain and snow fall from the clouds.

Melting snow and rain return to rivers and lakes.

evaporation
The sun's heat changes water into water vapor.

Sky Watch

Name_____

Weather changes. Will tomorrow's weather be like today's? Keep a weather chart for one week.

Record the weather in the morning and afternoon by drawing the correct pictures on the chart below.

rain   snow   sunny   cloudy   partly cloudy

Answers will vary.

This Week's Weather					
	Monday	Tuesday	Wednesday	Thursday	Friday
A. M.					
P. M.					

Answer Key

A Nice Day Outside
Name _____

We like to play outside on hot days, cold days and mild days.

Look at the temperature in each picture.

Write the temperature and **hot, cold** or **mild** to tell what kind of day each is.

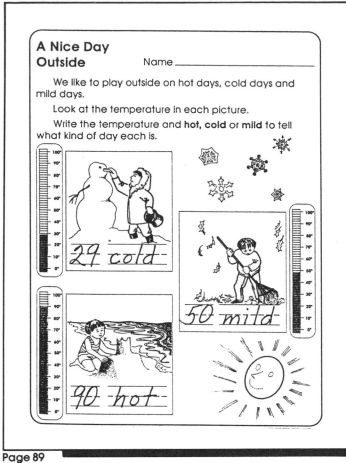

29 cold

50 mild

90 hot

Hot or Cold?
Name _____

A thermometer tells us the temperature. Make your own thermometer and practice reading the temperature.

1. Color the bottom half of the tube red.
2. Cut out the tube.
3. Cut the slits **A** and **B** on the thermometer.
4. Fold and insert the ends of the tube in slits **A** and **B**.
5. Slide the tube up or down and read the different temperatures.

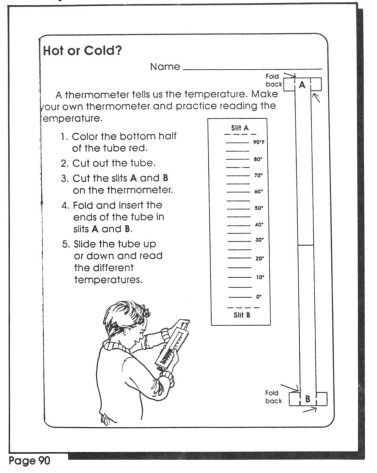

Lifting with Levers
Name _____

A lever is a simple machine used to lift or move things. It has two parts. The **arm** is the part that moves. The **fulcrum** supports the arm and does not move.

Name the parts of this lever.

force

load

fulcrum

Unscramble the names of these levers.

velosh
shovel

mrahem
hammer

moorb
broom

tun   reckarc
nut cracker

Levers at Work
Name _____

Levers help make our work easier. Circle all the levers. Then find their names in the wordsearch.

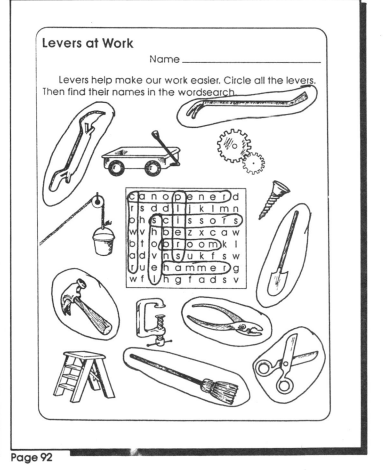

```
c a n o p e n e r d
r s d d l j k l m n
h s c i s s o r s
v h b e z x c a w
b t o b r o o m k l
a d v n s u k f s w
r u e h a m m e r g
w f l h g f a d s v
```

IF8757 Science Enrichment

Answer Key

The Wedge

Name _____

A wedge is a type of inclined plane. It is made up of two inclined planes joined together to make a sharp edge. A wedge can be used to cut things. Some wedges are pointed.

Color only the pictures of wedges.

Machines with a Slant

Name _____

An inclined plane has a slanted surface. It is used to move things from a low place to a high place. Some inclined planes are smooth. Others have steps.

Color the inclined planes in the picture.

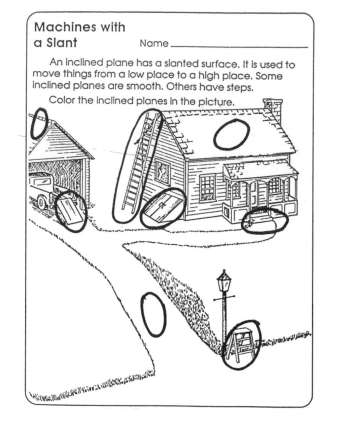

Screws

Name _____

A screw is a very helpful simple machine. It can be used to hold two pieces of wood together. It can not be pulled easily out of wood like a smooth nail.

1. Color part of the inclined plane as shown below.
2. Cut out the inclined plane.
3. Wrap it around a pencil as shown.
4. Tape it at the bottom.
5. Twirl the pencil with your fingers. What does it look like?

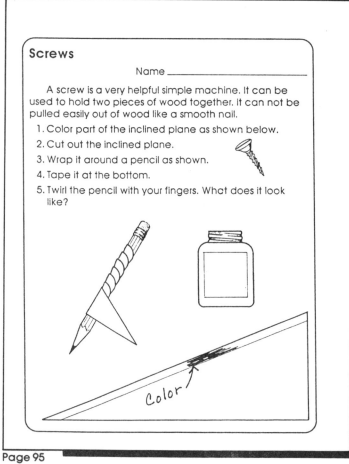

Color

Six Simple Machines

Name _____

Welcome to *Simon's Simple Machine Shop*. Simon needs some help putting his simple machines where they belong. Color and cut out each simple machine. Glue each one in the correct place.

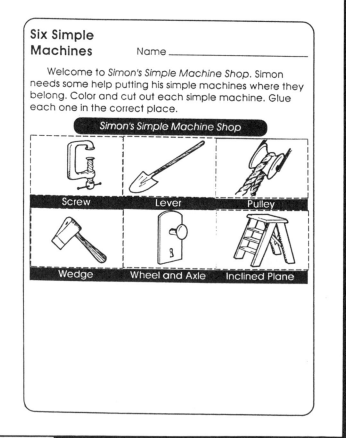

Simon's Simple Machine Shop

Screw	Lever	Pulley
Wedge	Wheel and Axle	Inclined Plane

IF8757 Science Enrichment

Answer Key

The Right Tool for the Job

Name _____

Mother gave Tyrone and Kim a list of jobs. Help them pick the right tool for each job. Draw a line from the job to the tool.

What will help Kim raise the flag up the flagpole?

What will Tyrone use to help him get the cat out of the tree.

What will Kim use to carry sand to her new sandbox?

What will Tyrone use to get the nail out of the board?

What will Kim use to hang the mirror on her bedroom door?

What will Tyrone use to slice the turkey?

inclined plane

pulley

lever

screw

wheel and axle

wedge

As Easy as 1 - 2 - 3!

Name _____

Machines make our work easier. There are many kinds of machines. Some machines are big and some are small. Some machines have many parts while some have just one.

Color and cut out the machines. Glue each one next to the picture that shows where it's needed on the Job Chart.

Job Chart

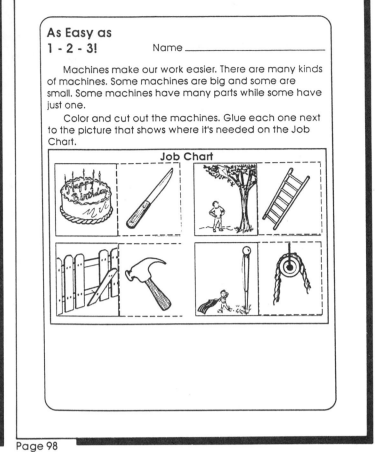

Who Am I?

Name _____

Use the words in the Tool Box to name the simple machine in each picture. Then you will find the answer to this question.

What do machines use to do work? _energy_

1. w h e e l + a x l e
2. i n c l i n e d p l a n e
3. l e v e r
4. s c r e w
5. w e d g e
6. p u l l e y

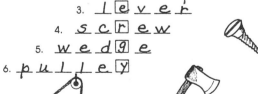

Tool Box

wheel & axle	inclined plane	screw
wedge	lever	pulley

Magnets Pull

Name _____

Draw a line from the magnet to each thing that it can pull.

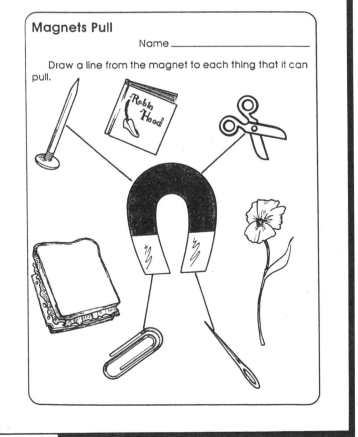

IF8757 Science Enrichment

Answer Key

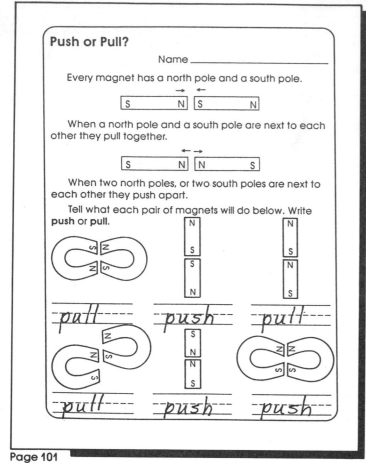

Push or Pull?

Name _____

Every magnet has a north pole and a south pole.

When a north pole and a south pole are next to each other they pull together.

When two north poles, or two south poles are next to each other they push apart.

Tell what each pair of magnets will do below. Write **push** or **pull**.

pull　*push*　*pull*

pull　*push*　*push*

Page 101

Sticky Hunt

Name _____

What things will a magnet stick to?

Make lists of the things in your room that will and will not stick to a magnet. *Answers will vary.*

Magnets stick to:	Magnets do not stick to:

Caution: Do not try your magnet on these things.

TV	Computer disks
VCR	Cassette tapes
Computer	Video tapes
Radio	Credit cards
Tape recorder	Telephone

Page 102

About the book . . .

This book will enhance your science program with entertaining, interesting and informative activities covering such diverse topics as insects, animals, trees, plants, the human body, nutrition, simple machines and weather.

About the author . . .

Daryl Vriesenga holds a Master's Degree from Michigan State University in Science Education. He has taught at the elementary level for over eighteen years. He is the author of several science books for the elementary classroom, including **Science Fair Projects**, **Science Activities**, **Earth Science** and **The Human Body**, among others.

Credits . . .

Author: Daryl Vriesenga
Editors: Jackie Servis and Sue Sutton
Artists: Sandra W. Ludwig and Ann Stein
Production: Pat Geasler and Sharon Kirkwood
Cover Photo: Dan Van Duinen